Effectiveness of Post-Fire Seeding at the Fitzner-Eberhardt Arid Land Ecology Reserve, Washington

By Troy A. Wirth and David A. Pyke

Prepared in cooperation with the U.S. Fish and Wildlife Service

Open-File Report 2011-1241

U.S. Department of the Interior
U.S. Geological Survey

U.S. Department of the Interior
KEN SALAZAR, Secretary

U.S. Geological Survey
Marcia K. McNutt, Director

U.S. Geological Survey, Reston, Virginia: 2011

For more information on the USGS—the Federal source for science about the Earth, its natural and living resources, natural hazards, and the environment, visit *http://www.usgs.gov* or call 1-888-ASK-USGS.

For an overview of USGS information products, including maps, imagery, and publications, visit *http://www.usgs.gov/pubprod*

To order this and other USGS information products, visit *http://store.usgs.gov*

Suggested citation:
Wirth, T.A., and Pyke, D.A. 2011, Effectiveness of post-fire seeding at the Fitzner-Eberhardt Arid Land Ecology Reserve, Washington: U.S. Geological Survey Open-File Report 2011-1241,42 p.

Contents

Figures

Tables

Conversion Factors and Datums

Conversion Factors

Multiply	By	To obtain
Length		
inch (in.)	2.54	centimeter (cm)
foot (ft)	0.3048	meter (m)
mile (mi)	1.609	kilometer (km)
Area		
acre	4,047	square meter (m^2)
acre	0.4047	hectare (ha)
acre	0.004047	square kilometer (km^2)
square foot (ft^2)	0.09290	square meter (m^2)
Volume		
ounce, fluid (fl. oz)	0.02957	liter (L)
Mass		
ounce, avoirdupois (oz)	28.35	gram (g)
pound, avoirdupois (lb)	0.4536	kilogram (kg)
Density		
plants per square meter (plants/m^2)	4,047	plants per acre (plants/acre)
plants per square meter (plants/m^2)	10,000	plants per hectare (plants/ha)

Active ingredient per acre (ai/acre) is the number of grams of biologically active herbicide applied per acre.

Temperature in degrees Celsius (°C) may be converted to degrees Fahrenheit (°F) as follows:
$$°F=(1.8×°C)+32.$$
Temperature in degrees Fahrenheit (°F) may be converted to degrees Celsius (°C) as follows:
$$°C=(°F-32)/1.8.$$

Datums

Vertical coordinate information is referenced to North American Vertical Datum of 1988 (NAVD 88).
Horizontal coordinate information is referenced to the North American Datum of 1983 (NAD 83).

Effectiveness of Post-Fire Seeding at the Fitzner-Eberhardt Arid Land Ecology Reserve, Washington

By Troy A. Wirth and David A. Pyke

Executive Summary

In August 2007, the Milepost 17 and Wautoma fires burned a combined total of 77,349 acres (31,302 hectares) of the Fitzner-Eberhardt Arid Land Ecology Reserve (ALE), part of the Hanford Reach National Monument administered by the U.S. Fish and Wildlife Service (USFWS) Mid-Columbia National Wildlife Refuge. In 2008, the USFWS implemented a series of seeding and herbicide treatments to mitigate potential negative consequences of these fires, including mortality of native vegetation, invasion of *Bromus tectorum* (cheatgrass), and soil erosion. Treatments included combinations of seeding (drill and aerial), herbicides, and one of six different mixtures of species. *Artemisia tridentata* ssp. *wyomingensis* (Wyoming big sagebrush) also was planted by hand in a small area in the southern end of the fire perimeter. Due to differences in plant communities prior to the fire and the multiple treatments applied, treatments were grouped into five treatment associations including mid-elevation aerial seedings, low-elevation aerial seedings, low-elevation drill seedings, high-elevation drill seeding, and no seeding treatments. Data collected at the mid-elevation aerial seedings indicate that the seeding did not appear to increase the density of seedlings compared to the non-seeded area in 2010. At the low-elevation aerial seedings, there were significantly more seedlings at seeded areas as compared to non-seeded areas. Low densities of existing perennial plants probably fostered a low-competition environment enabling seeds to germinate and emerge in 2010 during adequate moisture. Low-elevation drill seedings resulted in significant emergence of seeded grasses in 2009 and 2010 and forbs in 2010. This was likely due to adequate precipitation and that the drill seeding assured soil-to-seed contact. At the high-elevation drill seeding, which was implemented in 2009, there were a high number of seedlings in 2010. Transplanting of *A. tridentata* following the fires resulted in variable survival rates that warrant further testing; however, transplants located closer to washes tended to have the highest survival rates. Overall, the low-elevation aerial and drill seedings, and the high-elevation drill seedings resulted in significant numbers of seedlings. Further research is needed on methods that provide land managers with critical information about whether or not to seed post-fire areas including status of pre-fire vegetation and estimates of plant mortality due to fire.

Introduction

In August 2007, the Milepost 17 and Wautoma fires burned a combined total of 77,349 acres (31,302 ha) of the Fitzner-Eberhardt Arid Land Ecology Reserve (ALE), part of the Hanford Reach National Monument administered by the U.S. Fish and Wildlife Service (USFWS) Mid-Columbia National Wildlife Refuge (First Strike Environmental, 2007a, 2007b) (fig. 1). Burned areas were entirely within the perimeter of the 24 Command fire that occurred in 2000 (Evans and Lih, 2005). The wildfires of 2007 burned across a variety of soil types and vegetation communities from the flats of Cold Creek Valley to the northeastern slopes of Rattlesnake Mountain. Prior to the fire, plant communities within the area primarily were sagebrush grasslands in various conditions ranging from intact to degraded; however, most sagebrush had been removed during the 24 Command fire in 2000.

In 2008, the USFWS implemented a series of seeding and herbicide treatments to mitigate potential negative consequences of the 2007 fires, including mortality of native vegetation, invasion by the exotic annual grass *Bromus tectorum* (cheatgrass), and soil erosion (First Strike Environmental, 2007a, 2007b). Treatments included combinations of seeding (drill and aerial), herbicides (Plateau® at 4 oz/acre, Journey® at 6 or 11 oz/acre, or Milestone® at 6 oz/acre), and one of six different seedmixes (table 1; fig. 1). Due to the multiple treatments applied, treatments are coded as follows: Seeding type (A = aerial, D = drill, N = none), herbicide (J = Journey®, P = Plateau®, M = Milestone®, N = none), and rate of herbicide in ounces per acre followed by a dash with the seedmix type (1 through 6). For example, the DJ6-2 treatment was drill seeded with seedmix 2 and sprayed with Journey® herbicide at 6 oz/acre (table 1). *Artemisia tridentata ssp. wyomingensis* (Wyoming big sagebrush) also was planted by hand in a small area in the southern end of the fire perimeter in fall/winter 2008 (fig. 1).

Aerial spraying for all herbicide treatment combinations occurred between February 28 and March 9, 2008 using fixed-wing aircraft. Areas treated with Plateau® were deemed to be at risk for an increased abundance or invasion of cheatgrass, especially in areas where cheatgrass was not prevalent prior to the fire. In these areas, native bunchgrasses were relatively intact but had been burned more intensely in 2000 during the 24 Command fire. The active ingredient in Plateau® is imazapic, which can be applied as both a pre- and post-emergent herbicide that is readily absorbed by leaves and roots and translocated to meristematic tissue where it acts to inhibit synthesis of several amino acids. Imazapic is a selective herbicide depending on the species, timing, and rate of application (Tu and others, 2001). Imazapic has been effective at controlling cheatgrass and some other annual weeds, but also can cause some damage to mature perennial grasses and forbs (Tu and others, 2001; Kyser and others, 2007; Baker and others, 2009; Morris and others, 2009).

Areas treated with Journey® were deemed to be at a moderate (receiving 6 oz/acre) or high (receiving 11 oz/acre) risk of invasion or dominance by *B. tectorum* and where pre-existing bunchgrasses had not been burned as intensely in the 24 Command fire. Journey® contains the active ingredient imazapic as well as glyphosate (Roundup®), a non-selective herbicide. Journey® is used when suppression of actively growing and photosynthesizing vegetation at the time of spraying is desired or can be tolerated. For example, the combination of both herbicides will suppress vegetation at both the time of spraying, and imazapic will cause residual suppression of sensitive species. Milestone is a broadleaf specific herbicide that was sprayed for the control of *Chondrilla juncea* (rush skeletonweed) at ALE). Actual rates of active ingredients (ai) in each herbicide used on ALE were:

1. Plateau® 4 oz/acre: 0.06 lb imazapic ai/acre or 69.20 g ai/ha.
2. Journey® 6 oz/acre: 0.04 lb imazapic ai/acre or 39.20 g ai/ha and 0.07 lb glyphosate ai/acre or 78.74g ai/ha.
3. Journey® 11 oz/acre: 0.06 lb imazapic ai/acre or 72.10 g ai/ha and 0.13 lb glyphosate ai/acre or 144.42 g ai/ha.
4. Milestone® 6 oz/acre: 0.09 lb aminopyralid ai/acre or 105.00 g ai/ha.

The Plateau® at 4 oz/acre has a higher rate of imazapic than the Journey® 6 oz/acre treatment.

Drill seedings were applied on flat areas close to Washington State Route 240 where existing plant communities were less intact and abundance of *B. tectorum* was greater than areas where aerial seeding was applied. Three different models of drills were used (John Deere 455 (35 ft), Great Plains (12 ft), and a Laird (10 ft). Cultipackers were pulled behind each drill to firm the soil seedbed. Drill seedings were applied between mid-November 2008 and February 2009 with the exception of one area (DJ11-6), where application occurred in late fall 2009. Aerial seedings were applied with a fixed-wing aircraft on steeper slopes where pre-existing plant communities generally were more intact except for the absence of sagebrush. Aerial seedings were applied during the last week of November 2008.

Six seedmixes were applied to burned areas (table 2). Seedmixes 1 and 2 were applied to low elevation sandy or silt loam soils with degraded plant communities. Seedmix 1 had higher rates of *Achnatherum hymenoides* (Indian ricegrass) and *Elymus elymoides* (bottlebrush squirreltail) than seedmix 2 and was applied only over a very small area. Seedmix 2 was similar to seedmix 1 but had a lower overall rate due to the large area of application. Seedmix 3 was applied over a large area of silt loam soils with mostly intact plant communities composed primarily of *Poa secunda* (Sandberg's bluegrass), *A. hymenoides* and *Pseudoroegneria spicata* (bluebunch wheatgrass). Seedmix 3 differed from seedmix 4 in that it had roughly twice the rate of *P. secunda* and *P. spicata*. Areas treated with seedmix 4 were deemed to have high densities of *P. secunda* and *P. spicata* before the fire than after the fire and, therefore, seedmix 4 included lower rates of these species. Seedmix 5 was applied to an area of loamy sand, whereas seedmix 6 was applied to a high-elevation portion of Snively Basin that was historically converted to *Secale cereale* (cereal rye).

In December 2007, bare-root sagebrush seedlings were planted within a small portion of the burned area (fig. 1). Transplants received one of three different treatments (Plant Success™ tablets, MycoApply® root dip, TerraSorb® fine hydrogel) or were untreated, and one of two spacings (15 or 4 ft). Plant Success™ tablets were added into the hole at the time of transplanting. Plant Success™ tablets contain multiple species of mycorrhizal fungi and fertilizer and are designed to increase plant growth and survival by enhancing mycorrhizal colonization. MycoApply® root dip is a similar product that contains mycorrhizae except that roots were dipped in the mixture prior to planting. TerraSorb® fine hydrogel consists of granules of potassium polyacrylamide acrylate copolymers that capture moisture when it is available and slowly releases it over time as the soil dries. One pound of TerraSorb® fine hydrogel was mixed with 25 gallons of water, and the roots of each transplant were dipped in the slurry prior to planting (approximately 90 mg of medium per transplant with some variation in the amount due to transplant size and handling). Those areas receiving 4 ft (0.047 plants/m^2) spacing were located linearly along washes, whereas those planted with a spacing of 15 ft (0.67 plants/m^2) were located in upland areas.

The objectives of treatments applied on ALE were to mitigate the potential negative consequences of these fires, including invasion of exotic annual plants and loss of existing perennial plants. Herbicides were applied to reduce the risk of exotic annual grass abundance and invasion, and seed was applied to establish new plants that would replace plants lost to fire and also to enhance degraded plant communities. The density of seeded plants is the best measure of seeding effectiveness in the first several years after a fire. Monitoring fluctuations of cover and density of annual plants after treatment can help explain patterns of seeding success. In order to measure these objectives, USGS monitored density and cover of vegetation within each of the treatments in 2009 and 2010, with special emphasis on seedlings and exotic annual plants.

Monitoring Methods

Seed traps were placed during aerial seeding in fall 2008 to verify that proposed seed rates were applied. Aluminum trays (36 × 26 cm) lined with contact adhesive-coated paper were placed within areas to be treated. Seeds trapped within each tray were sorted by species and viability (hard, filled seeds) and used to estimate the actual seeding rate of the aerially treated areas. The measured seeding rate was lower than the target rate for all seedmixes (table 3). Seed traps were located just prior to the aerial seeding and collected no more than 1 day later; however, it is possible that some seeds bounced out of the seed traps or that some were removed by rodents.

In spring 2009 and 2010, 127 vegetation monitoring plots were placed within treated areas of the Milepost 17 and Wautoma fires within ALE (table A1). Permanent plots were placed randomly within each treatment/herbicide combination. At each plot, three 50-m transects were established 5 m from the plot center and spaced 120° from each other in a spoke design (Herrick and others, 2005). Photographs were taken from the plot center pointing outward along each transect and also at 25 m pointing toward the ground. These were used to document the vegetation and soil surface conditions of each transect. Along each transect, plant densities of perennial grasses and seeded forbs were recorded by counting the number of each plant species in 10, 0.5-m^2 quadrats spaced 5 m apart. In 2010, seedlings were categorized as perennial grass, wheatgrass, needlegrass[1], or *P. secunda*. For aerial seedings, all seedlings were called "seedlings" because seedlings from the treatments and from naturally occurring plants could not be distinguished. For drill seedings, seedlings occurring in drill rows were called "seeded" because they could be identified as resulting from the treatments. In 2009, all seedling grasses were classified as seedling perennial grasses because identification to species was uncertain. Seedling forbs were identified to species in 2009 and 2010. Stem density of *B. tectorum* and density of *S. kali* individuals were counted within 0.04-m^2 (20 × 20 cm) subquadrats within each 0.5-m^2 quadrat. Density of less-common perennial grasses and shrubs were counted in 2 × 50-m belt transects in the aerial seedings and 3 × 50-m belt transects in the drill seedings. In 2010, density of perennial grasses within the 0.5-m^2 quadrats was only recounted if there was an apparent difference in the number from 2009. Density within belt transects was not repeated in 2010 to maximize the amount of field time spent searching for seedlings. Cover of vegetation was collected using the line-point intercept technique in which 100 points were collected along each transect (every 0.5 m), resulting in 300 points collected per plot (Herrick and others, 2005).

---

[1] Needlegrass is a common name for three species in two genera. The common name is used throughout this report because the species could not be differentiated as seedlings.

Eight aerial control plots (AC) were established outside of the aerially seeded area in 2010 in an attempt to assess natural seedling emergence; however, there were few locations that could be considered equivalent to the aerially seeded areas. Most AC plots were higher than the mid-elevation aerial seedings and were representative of an intact plant community. Two low-elevation AC plots were invaded by *B. tectorum* and not representative of most aerially seeded areas. They were, therefore, excluded from comparisons (AC-5 and AC-6). Additionally, six plots at the NJ6-N were not seeded and could be potentially used as controls but lacked the deep-rooted perennial grass component characteristic of most aerially seeded areas (tables A2 and A3).

Monitoring plots for transplants were established in late October 2008, and were subsequently monitored in June 2009 and June 2010. Sagebrush transplants in the treatments using 15 ft spacing were monitored using the same plot selection and design as for the seeding and herbicide treatments except that only belt transects were collected. Each belt transect was 12×50-m in size, resulting in the sampling of 1,800-m^2 per plot. The number of live sagebrush transplants was counted within each transect. Plantings using the 4 ft spacing were linear and not wide enough to be monitored using the three-transect spoke design. Therefore, for the 4 ft plantings, single transects were established parallel to washes to monitor transplant survival. Because monitoring of transplants began in October 2008, initial plant densities of 0.047 and 0.67 plants/m^2 in the 15 and 4 ft spacing treatments were assumed.

Analyses

Statistical analysis was conducted using the R statistical language (R Development Core Team, 2010). Most of the data were positively skewed, resulting in means that overestimated vegetation cover and density. To adjust for this, data were log transformed for analyses, and medians are presented in graphs and tables rather than means. Significance (α-level) for all statistical tests was 0.1.

Due to differences in plant communities prior to the fire and the multiple treatments applied, treatments were grouped into five treatment associations (table 4):

1. mid-elevation aerial seedings,
2. low-elevation aerial seedings,
3. low-elevation drill seedings,
4. high elevation drill seeding, and
5. no seeding treatments.

The mid-elevation aerial seedings consisted of treatments AJ6-3 (n=11), AJ6-4 (n=5), AP4-3 (n=14), AP4-4 (n=5), ANN-4 (n=5), AP4-1 (n=3), and AJ6-1 (n=5) (table 4). The AC plots established in 2010 were used to compare the effectiveness of these aerial seedings in establishing seedlings, and the ANN-4 plots were used to assess the effectiveness of herbicides. A one-way analysis of variance (ANOVA) was used to test for differences among groups, followed by a Dunnett's test to test for differences between each group and the reference (AC or ANN-4). Due to initial differences in areas receiving the different treatments, direct comparisons among all treatments could not be made, and no statistical comparisons were made among different seedmixes.

The low-elevation aerial seedings consisted of the AJ11-1 (n=3) and AJ11-2 (n=5) treatments. To evaluate effectiveness for these treatments, the AJ11-1 and AJ11-2 treatments were compared to DJ11-2 no-drill plots. An ANOVA was used to test for differences between groups, followed by a Dunnett's test to test between each of the seeded and non-seeded treatments. The same type and rate of herbicide were used on all three of the low-elevation treatments, and there were no suitable controls; therefore, no statistical analyses were performed for effects of herbicide on the low-elevation aerial seedings. The low-elevation drill seeding treatments consisted of DJ6-2 (control n=8, treatment n=7), DJ11-2 (control n=9, treatment n=11), and DP4-5 (control n=3, treatment n=3). Treatment plots were compared to control plots using a Welch 2 sample t-test for unequal sample sizes and variances using log-transformed data. No-drill plots from DJ11-2 were compared to treatment plots for DJ11-1 because DJ11-1 was too small to have no-drill plots. The high-elevation drill seeding treatment consisted only of the DJ11-6 (n=3) seeding conducted in late fall/early winter 2009, and the no-seeding treatments included NJ6-N (n=6) and NM6-N (n=3). For the high-elevation drill seeding and no-seeding treatments, data are presented but statistical comparisons were not conducted.

To evaluate the effectiveness of the different herbicide applications, the change in cheatgrass densities from 2009 to 2010 were compared to either a control (for aerial seedings, the ANN-4 treatment), or between each of the individual drill treatments because there were no controls for the herbicide application at the drill seedings. An ANOVA, followed by Dunnett's test was used for this analysis (table 4).

Transplant survival by treatment compared the original densities planted in fall/winter 2007 to densities measured at subsequent monitoring in 2008, 2009, and 2010. No statistical tests were performed because of the uncertainty regarding initial transplant numbers, different plot designs, and low sample sizes.

Results and Discussion

Site Conditions

Average annual precipitation in this area is approximately 6.8 in/yr. Precipitation after seeding was close to average from December 2008 through April 2009, followed by a 5-month period (May–September 2009) during which each month received less than 40 percent of the long-term average precipitation (1981–2010; fig. 2). These are typically dry months in this region. Fall/winter 2009–10 were relatively dry with 4 of 6 months receiving less than average precipitation. Late spring 2010 was wet, with May and June 2010 having more than twice the long-term average precipitation. Weather data were obtained from the Hanford meteorological station, which is located northwest of ALE on the Hanford Nuclear Reservation.

Pre-fire vegetation communities within aerially seeded portions of ALE consisted of relatively diverse mixtures of deep- and shallow-rooted grass species, perennial forbs, and biological soil crusts, along with low densities of invasive annuals *(B. tectorum* and *S. kali)* (Evans and Lih, 2005). Deep-rooted perennial grasses consisted primarily of *P. spicata, A. hymenoides, Heterostipa comata* (needle-and-thread grass), *Acnatherum thurberianum* (Thurbers needlegrass) and *Poa cusickii* (Cusick's bluegrass). Shallow-rooted grass species consisted overwhelmingly of *P. secunda* and, occasionally, *Poa bulbosa* (bulbous bluegrass). Over the entire aerially seeded area, in 2009 and 2010, there was a mean density of 43.6 shallow-rooted and 2.25 deep-rooted perennial grass plants/m^2 (table 4). The predominant soil types were silt loams in aerially seeded portions, with the exceptions of AJ11-1 and AJ11-2. These two treatments had a lower abundance of perennial grasses and generally sandy soils (table A1).

In contrast, drill-seeded areas consisted of less perennial grass and biological soil crusts along with a higher abundance of invasive annuals than aerially seeded portions (table 5). Drill-seeded areas consisted of a mixture of silt loam and sandy soil types (table A1).

6

Within aerial seeding treatments, fire-induced mortality of pre-existing perennial grass plants appeared to be low. Few dead bunchgrasses were observed during monitoring in 2009 and 2010. Within the entire treated area, there was a decrease in densities of *B. tectorum* from 2009 to 2010 (table 5). In 2009, *B. tectorum* plants were small and stunted, although very dense, possibly due to a wet winter followed by a very dry spring. Residual effects of the 2008 herbicide application also may have had an effect. In 2010, there were much lower densities of *B. tectorum*, but because of the wet spring, plants were much larger and produced more seeds than in 2009. Densities of *S. kali* were more variable with an overall decrease in the drill seedings, and a slight increase in the aerial seedlings from 2009 to 2010.

Some effects of herbicides were noted that were not apparent in the density or cover data. These effects were dramatic in some areas that were dominated by *B. tectorum* prior to the fire. A shift from *B. tectorum* to bare ground was observed at some locations with unstable soils (fig. 3a). In these areas, soil loss due to wind and apparent mortality of *P. secunda* was observed (fig. 3b). It is unknown whether or not this mortality of *P. secunda* was due to the fire, herbicide, post-fire erosion, or a combination of all three factors. Throughout herbicide areas, but especially in areas with high *B. tectorum* abundance, a visible banding pattern of vegetation dominance was observed. This banding was the result of alternating predominance of *B. tectorum* or perennial grasses and *S. kali* (fig. 3c). It is uncertain if areas dominated by *S. kali* (fig. 3c, green bands) were areas that received the full herbicide rate and the other (fig. 3c, brown bands) a lesser rate, or if the areas evident as green bands received a higher rate than the adjacent areas evident as brown bands. In some areas, it appeared as if there was mortality of *P. secunda* within bands dominated by *S. kali* (fig. 3d). Mortality of *P. secunda* also has been observed by Bekedam (2004) within sagebrush steppe treated with Imazapic. In addition, Kyser and others (2007), working in northern California and southeastern Oregon, observed a shift from dominance of annual grass species to broadleaf species after application of imazapic. They found generally less vegetation cover with increasing rates of imazapic (ranging from 35 to 210 g ae/ha) (Kyser and others, 2007). *S. kali* germinates later in the season than *B. tectorum*, so in locations where *B. tectorum* was absent due to the herbicide, *S. kali* had less competition. Additionally, the later germination of *S. kali* may have allowed it to escape any damaging effects of glyphosate.

Cover of perennial grasses generally was lower in 2010 despite increased water availability at aerial- and drill-seeded treatments (figs. 4a, 4b, 5a, and 5b). This effect is most apparent at aerial-seeded areas due to the initial abundance of perennial grasses. Below normal precipitation in 2009 may have influenced the cover of perennial grasses in 2010 by causing reduced tillering, resulting in less leaf area the following year (Brown, 1995) or it is possible that herbicides could have damaged growth, but not survival of existing perennial grasses (Shinn and Thill, 2004). Cover of *B. tectorum* also decreased in most treatments from 2009 to 2010 (figs. 4c and 5c), with the exception of DJ6-2 and AJ11-2. Cover of *S. kali* was variable, decreasing in some treatments, and increasing in others (figs. 4d and 5d). Additionally, increases in cover of biological soil crusts were recorded from 2009 to 2010. This was because these crusts were easier to identify when conditions were moist, as they often were in the spring of 2010 (Table A4). Litter cover was variable, increasing at sites in 2010 with high vegetative cover and decreasing at sites with low cover (for example, AJ11-1, AJ11-2, and AP4-1) (Table A4). Bare ground within the aerial seedings was similar in 2009 and 2010 except for AJ6-1 where there was a 14 percent decrease and AJ11-2 where there was a 12 percent increase in bare ground (Table A4). For drill seedings, several treatments increased bare ground by 10 percent or greater (DJ6-2 and DP4-5 drill plots). Bare ground at the DJ11-1 drill plots increased by 35 percent. Bare ground at the NJ6-N no-seeding treatments was generally the same from 2009 to 2010 (tables A4 and A5).

Mid-Elevation Aerial Seedings

The mid-elevation aerial seedings (AJ6-3, AJ6-4, ANN-4, AP4-3, AP4-4, AP4-1, and AJ6-1) encompassed most of the treated area (18,209 acres). These treatments had a large component of pre-existing shallow- and deep-rooted perennial grasses (fig. 6a).

In 2009, there were few seedlings found, but in 2010, there was significant emergence of both grass and forb seedlings (fig. 6b). In 2010, seedling grasses emerged differently by site (ANOVA, $F_{(7, 46)}$ = 2.97, p=0.01). Treatments AJ6-1 and AJ6-3 had significantly lower emergence of seedling grasses than the non-seeded site (AC) (Dunnett's test, p=0.04 and 0.02, respectively). All other treatments were not different from the non-seeded plots (Dunnett's test, p>0.01). Composition of seedling grasses at seeded sites primarily were *P. spicata* (89.5 percent), with a small amount of *P. secunda* (4.6 percent) and needlegrasses (3.1 percent).

Several aerial treatments showed higher densities of seeded forbs (primarily *A. millefolium*) than the control site (fig. 6b); however, due to a high amount of variability in the data and low sample size in some treatments (for example, AP4-1 had only three plots due to its small size), there were no significant differences between sites (ANOVA, $F_{(7, 46)}$ = 1.35, p=0.24). Seedmix 3 had a higher rate of *A. millefolium* than seedmix 4, which may have contributed to the variability. Additionally, different densities of pre-existing *A. millefolium* in the different treatments probably further affected the seedling densities. Although densities of pre-existing *A. millefolium* generally were low, ANN-4 had the highest (median density of 0.045 plants/m^2), and AP4-1 and AJ6-1 had median densities of 0.016 and 0.013 plants/m^2, respectively.

Decreases in median density of *B. tectorum* occurred at all treated sites from 2009 to 2010. The site that received no herbicide treatment (ANN-4) also showed a decrease (fig. 6c). Cover of *B. tectorum* also decreased correspondingly (fig. 4c). Densities of *S. kali* increased at most treatments from 2009 to 2010 (AJ6-1, AJ6-3, AP4-3, and AP4-4), although decreasing in the AP4-1 treatment. There was only a slight decrease in *S. kali* density at the no-herbicide (ANN-4) treatment and at AJ6-4, but these treatments had low initial densities in 2009 (fig. 6d). Cover of *S. kali* showed generally similar patterns to the changes in density (fig. 4d).

Two levels of herbicides were used within the mid-elevation aerial seedings, Plateau® at 4 oz/ acre and Journey® at 6 oz/acre. Areas receiving the Plateau® and Journey® herbicides had nearly equal densities of shallow- and deep-rooted perennial grasses, although the area receiving no herbicide (ANN-4) had somewhat higher densities of shallow-and deep-rooted perennial grasses (fig. 7a). Densities of seedling perennial grasses were significantly different among treatments (ANOVA, $F_{(2, 51)}$ = 2.73, p= 0.07) in 2010. Seedling perennial grasses were higher in Plateau®-treated areas than in Journey®-treated areas in 2010 (median density of 3.17 seedlings/m^2 in Plateau® 4 oz/acre and 1.2 seedings/m^2 in the Journey® 6 oz/acre) but both had significantly lower densities than the no-herbicide treatment (6.0 seedlings/m^2, fig. 7b, Dunnett's test = p<0.01 for both the Journey® and Plateau® treatments). The herbicide possibly inhibited germination of perennial grass seedlings in the treated areas. There were no differences in seeded forbs among treatments (ANOVA, $F_{(2, 51)}$ = 0.32, p=0.72) (fig. 7b).

Median densities of *B. tectorum* decreased in all herbicide treatments from 2009 to 2010 (fig. 7c). Median density of *B. tectorum* decreased by 95 percent in the Plateau® treatment, 82 percent in the Journey® treatment, and 48 percent in the non-herbicide treatment (ANN-4). To account for the differences in initial densities, analyses were conducted using the proportional decreases in *B. tectorum* by treatment from 2009 to 2010. The proportional decrease in *B. tectorum* density from 2009 to 2010 was significant (ANOVA, $F_{(2, 44)}$ = 18.15, p=<0.01). Both treatments receiving Plateau® and Journey® had a significantly greater decrease in *B. tectorum* from 2009 to 2010 than the ANN-4 plots (Dunnett's test, p<0.01 for both treatments).

Median cover of *B. tectorum* decreased by 82, 61.5, and 20 percent in the Plateau® 4 oz, Journey® 6 oz, and no-herbicide treatments from 2009 to 2010. Differences among treatments were statistically significant (ANOVA, $F_{(2,41)}$ = 3.14 , p=0.05). Sites receiving Plateau® at a rate of 4 oz/acre showed a statistically significant decrease in *B. tectorum* cover from 2009 to 2010 compared to the ANN-4 plots (Dunnett's test, p=0.06), whereas those receiving Journey® at a rate of 6 oz/acre did not (Dunnett's test, p=0.73).

As previously discussed, the Plateau® treatment of 4 oz/acre contained a higher amount of the active ingredient imazapic than the Journey 6 oz/acre treatment. The Plateau® 4 oz/acre treatment may have reduced *B. tectorum* to a greater extent than the lower rate of imazapic with the addition of glyphosate in the Journey® 6 oz/acre treatment, but *B. tectorum* densities decreased significantly in both treatments from 2009 to 2010. In addition to the herbicide, the difference in weather between the 2 years likely also affected the observed densities of *B. tectorum*.

Density of *S. kali* increased in the Plateau® and Journey® treatments by 48 and 1,200 percent, respectively, from 2009 to 2010 (fig. 7d). Densities of *S. kali* in plots receiving herbicide were higher than the no-herbicide treatment (ANN-4) in 2010, although these plots had very little *S. kali* to begin with. Increases in the density of *S. kali* in 2010 could be due to the lack of competition with *B. tectorum*. Cover of these exotic annual species showed similar patterns, with *B. tectorum* decreasing and *S. kali* increasing from 2009 to 2010 in the two different herbicide treatments (fig. 4c and 4d). *S. kali* may have escaped the effect of glyphosate because significant germination of this species likely occurred after herbicide application.

Data collected at the mid-elevation aerial seedings indicate that:

1. There were equal amounts of seedlings in seeded and unseeded areas.

2. Within seeded areas, there were likely some emerging plants from the seeding, but it was not possible to distinguish between seeded and unseeded plants.

3. The seeding did not appear to increase the density of perennial seedlings compared to the non-seeded area in 2010.

4. Seed production from the pre-existing plant community was sufficient to produce substantial perennial seedlings in 2010.

Low-Elevation Aerial Seedings

The low-elevation aerial seedings consisted of the AJ11-1 and AJ11-2 treatments and covered 948 acres of the treated area within ALE. These treatments were different from the mid-elevation aerial seedings not only by being at lower elevations, but also, soils at AJ11-1 and AJ11-2 generally are sandy as opposed to the silt loams found at the mid-elevation aerial seedings (table A-1).

Median densities of pre-existing perennial grasses within the low-elevation aerial seedings were lower than mid-elevation aerial seedings. AJ11-2 had higher densities of shallow- and deep-rooted perennial grasses than AJ11-1 or the DJ11-2 no-drill plots (fig. 8a). In 2010, seedling grasses were found at significantly different densities among treatments (ANOVA, $F_{(2,14)}$ = 12.87, p<0.01) (fig. 8b).

In 2010, both AJ11-1 and AJ11-2 had significantly higher densities of seeded grasses than the DJ11-2 control plots (Dunnett's tests p=0.01 and 0.00 for AJ11-1 and AJ11-2, respectively). Compositions of seeded grasses within both the AJ11-1 and AJ11-2 were *P. secunda* (61.3 percent), *P. spicata* (23.1 percent), needlegrasses (12.2 percent), and 3.3 percent unknown perennial grass.

Densities of seeded forbs were not significantly different among treatments (ANOVA, $F_{(2,14)}$ = 2.52, p=0.12), despite the fact that differences appeared considerable (fig. 8b). This is due to the large amount of variability in the data, which reduced the ability to detect statistical differences.

In 2010, density of *B. tectorum* was lower than 2009 (fig. 8c) at the low-elevation aerial seeding treatments. Densities of *S. kali* also decreased from 2009 to 2010 in all the low-elevation aerial seeding treatments (fig. 8d). All areas received herbicide so we could not compare changes in *B. tectorum* and *S. kali* from 2009 to 2010 to an untreated area.

Data collected at the low-elevation aerial seedings suggest that there were significantly more seedlings at seeded areas in comparison to non-seeded areas for both AJ11-1 and AJ11-2. Low densities of existing perennial plants probably fostered a low-competition environment, enabling seeds to germinate and emerge in 2010 during adequate moisture.

Low-Elevation Drill Seedings

The low-elevation drill seedings consisted of the DJ11-1, DJ11-2, DJ6-2, and DP4-5 treatments These treatments covered 6,291 acres of the total treatment area. No-drill plots were established at all the low-elevation drill seedings, with the exception of DJ11-1 due to its small size. The no-drill plots were established after herbicide application so cannot be used for assessing herbicide effectiveness.

Densities of pre-existing shallow- and deep-rooted perennial grasses were variable among treatments, but generally were much less than aerially seeded treatments (fig. 9a). For all treatments, there were significantly higher densities of seeded grasses at drilled plots than at no-drill plots in 2009 and 2010 (p<0.01) and seeded forbs in 2010 (p=0.06). This pattern held across all treatments, likely due to higher precipitation in 2010.

The DJ11-2 drilled plots had significant emergence of seeded grasses in 2009 (0.87 versus 0.0 plants/m^2, t=10.17, p<0.01) and 2010 (5.87 drill versus 0.2 plants/m^2, t =5.89, p<0.01, figs. 9b and 9c). In 2010, most seedling seeded grasses were classified as *P. secunda* (85.3 percent), with the others classified as 6.5 percent *P. spicata*, 3.0 percent needlegrasses, and 5.1 percent unknown perennial grasses. Seedmix 2 contained a high seeding rate for *P. secunda,* which likely explains the dominance of this species in the emerging seedlings. There were no differences between drill and no-drill plots for seeded forbs in 2009 or 2010. All emerging forbs were *A. millefolium*.

Similar to the DJ11-2 treatment, the DJ6-2 treatment had significantly higher densities of seedling grasses in drill plots compared to no-drill plots in 2009 and 2010 (t = 3.63, p<0.01, 1.4 versus 0 plants/m^2 in 2009 and t=4.48, p<0.01, 5.8 versus 0.07 plants/m^2 in 2010) (figs. 9b and 9c). Seeded grasses were 41 percent *P spicata*, 34.4 percent *P. secunda*, 10.3 percent needlegrasses, and 12.3 percent unknown. There were no significant differences between seeded forbs at the drill versus no-drill plots in 2009 and 2010. Most seeded forbs were *A. millefolium* and rarely *L. perenne*.

There also were significantly higher densities of seeded grasses at drill plots than at no-drill plots at the DP4-5 in 2009 and 2010 (t = 18.59, p<0.01 in 2009 and t=3.38, p=0.02 in 2010). In 2009, there were 1.33 versus 0 plants/m^2, and in 2010, there were 1.93 versus 0.4 plants/m^2 in the drill and no-drill plots (figs. 9b and 9c). Grass seedling composition was 31.5 percent *P. secunda*, 29.3 percent unknown perennial grass, 25.8 percent needlegrass, and 13.3 percent *P. spicata*. There was very little forb germination in either year at the DP4-5 treatment area (fig. 9d).

Drill plots at the DJ11-1 were compared to the DJ11-2 no-drill plots because the DJ11-1 treatment area was too small to include no-drill plots. In 2009, there were no differences in seeded grasses and forbs at the drill versus no-drill plots. In contrast, in 2010 there were significant differences for both seeded grasses (t = 5.03, p<0.01, 3.07 versus 0.07 plants/m^2) and seeded forbs (t = 5.57, p<0.01, 5.73 versus 0 plants/m^2). Seeded grass composition was 59.2 percent *P. secunda*, 29.2 percent *P. spicata*, 6.9 percent unknown perennial grass, 4.6 percent needlegrass. All seeded forbs that emerged were *A. millefolium*.

All three levels of herbicide were included in the lower elevation drill-seeding treatments. There were no areas that did not receive herbicide that could be used as a suitable herbicide control. In 2009 and 2010, there were no differences between the herbicide treatments in terms of grass seedlings (ANOVA, $F_{(2,22)}$ = 0.11 in 2009 and 0.49 in 2010, p>0.1, fig. 10a). In 2009, there was also no differences for seeded forbs among herbicide treatments (ANOVA, $F_{(2, 22)}$ = 0.37, p=0.69). In 2010, there was a difference between herbicide treatments for seeded forbs (ANOVA, $F_{(2,22)}$ = 2.65, p=0.09) due to no forb seedlings being found in the DP4-5 treatment (fig. 10b). The lack of forb seedlings in this treatment could potentially be due to the herbicide, but sandy soils, which were subject to redistribution by wind, also could have been a factor.

Decreases in the median density of *B. tectorum* between 2009 and 2010 (treatment and no-drill plots combined) were 91.6, 51.3, and 73.0 percent in the Plateau[®] 4 oz/acre, Journey[®] 6 oz/acre, and Journey[®] 11 oz/acre treatments, respectively. Overall, decreases were large, but were not significantly different between treatments (ANOVA, $F_{(2,41)}$ = 2.27, p=0.11). Despite large decreases in density, decreases in cover from 2009 to 2010 were modest (fig. 5c). Larger plants appeared to compensate for the decrease in density.

Based on the data from the low-elevation drill seedings:

1. The low-elevation drill seedings resulted in significant emergence of seeded grasses in 2009 and 2010 and of forbs in 2010.

2. In 2009, assuring soil-to-seed contact by drill seeding likely increased germination whereas germination was likely suppressed for the aerial seedings where seeds were placed on the soil surface.

In 2010, adequate moisture promoted significant germination in low-elevation drill seedings. It is unknown what the survival of these seedlings will be in the future. It is normal for a die-off period to occur after initial emergence.

High-Elevation Drill Seeding

The drill seeding in the high-elevation Snively Basin was delayed until fall 2009. This 700 acre area was previously used for *S. cereale* (annual rye) production and the vegetation prior to treatment was composed primarily of *S. cereale* and a low number of *P. secunda* (11.9 plants/m^2). This area received Journey[®] herbicide at the rate of 11 oz/acre at the same time as the other treatments (February 2008) and additional chemical treatments in May 2009 and November 2009. It also was burned again intentionally in November 2009 to help control *S. cereale*.

In 2010, coincident with the above average precipitation, there were a high number of seedlings (table A3). There were an estimated 60.9 grass and 48.8 forb seedlings/m^2 in spring 2010. Forb seedlings primarily were *A. millefolium*, many of which were likely naturally occurring rather than seeded. This seeding also had a relatively high density of *B. tectorum* at 165.8 plants/m^2, but no *S. kali*. Based on the initial densities, the potential for establishment of seeded species is high, even with high seedling mortality rates.

No Seeding Treatments

The no-seeding treatments NM6-N and NJ6-N covered an area of 2,660 acres. Within the two no-seeding treatments, there were very low densities of deep-rooted perennial grasses, but medium to high densities of shallow rooted perennial grasses (fig. 11a). There were no seeded grasses found in 2009, but similar to the AC plots in 2010, there were some emerging non-seeded seedlings in 2010 (fig. 11b), likely due to favorable moisture conditions. There were more grass seedlings found in the NJ6-N treatment, which had higher densities of shallow-rooted grasses and lower densities of *B. tectorum* than the NM6-N treatment (fig. 11c). The density of *B. tectorum* at NJ6-N, which received Journey® herbicide at 6 oz/acre, decreased from 2009 to 2010, whereas NM6-N, which received Milestone® herbicide (broadleaf specific), showed an increase in *B. tectorum* density during the same time period. This provides some evidence that the herbicides Journey® and Plateau®, even though they were applied 2 years earlier, were having significant residual effects on the *B. tectorum* populations. *S. kali* densities in these two treatments increased slightly, but not significantly from 2009 to 2010 (fig. 11d).

NM6-N was located near State Highway 240 and was heavily infested with *B. tectorum*, yet it did not burn during the 2007 fires. Figure 3a shows the boundary between the non-burned and burned (*B. tectorum*-infested) area, and an adjacent area that also was dominated by *B. tectorum* prior to the fire but was burned and treated with Journey® at 11 oz/acre. Without herbicide, the community in the burned area likely would look similar to the unburned community after 1 or 2 years of recovery. However, with the suppression of *B. tectorum*, there is high cover of bare ground and evidence of soil movement due to wind is apparent.

Transplants

The initial planting densities for sagebrush transplants were 0.047 plants/m^2 (15-ft spacing) and 0.67 plants/m^2 (4-ft spacing) (table 6). Performance of transplants can be examined in two ways—comparing densities of plants at the time of each monitoring to the initial planting density or comparing densities of plants from the first monitoring period to subsequent monitoring periods. From the initial planting in December 2007 to the first monitoring in October 2008, plant density decreased from 5.5 to 48.9 percent of the initial densities (table 6). Decreases were greatest in the two treatments where plants were spaced at 4 ft. Of the remaining treatments, the TerraSorb® fine hydrogel with the 15-ft spacing had the lowest percentage of initial density (34 percent), whereas the MycoApply® root dip 15 ft had the highest percentage (48.9 percent).

Changes in density from October 2008 to June 2009 were different between treatments, with the Terrasorb® fine hydrogel with 15-ft spacing having the lowest survival (25 percent). The control 15 ft, MycoApply® root dip 15 ft, and Plant Success™ tablets 15 ft had survival rates of less than 50 percent from October 2008 to June 2009, whereas the 4 ft spacing treatments had the highest survival (93.9 and 64.9 percent for the Terrasorb® fine hydrogel and control, respectively). In contrast survival was lowest in the TerraSorb® fine hydrogel 4 ft and control 4 ft treatments (4.6 and 3.6 percent, respectively) when compared to the original densities, and highest for the Plant Success™ tablets 15 ft (21.2 percent).

From June 2009 to June 2010, survival was greater than the previous 2 years, ranging from 60 to 100 percent. Despite having an overall low survival rate during the entire period, the TerraSorb® fine hydrogel 15 ft did not show any decrease from 2009 to 2010, while all other treatments had some losses. A favorable moisture year combined with plants that were probably relatively well established were likely factors in a higher survival rate during this time period.

Comparing final densities in 2010 to the first monitoring in 2008, the two treatments with the highest survival rates were treatments that received the 4 ft-spacing (control 4 ft and TerraSorb® fine hydrogel 4 ft with 45.9 and 75.8 percent survival, respectively). The location of the 4-ft spacing treatments (near washes) may have been a factor responsible for the higher survival of transplants in the high-density treatments. However, there were fewer plots that received this treatment and variation was higher because of the smaller sample size (table 6). Additionally, this result may have occurred because of the particular weather patterns experienced during the monitoring period. For instance, survival from 2009 to 2010 was much higher (a wet period) than survival from 2008 to 2009 (a dry period).

When comparing the initial planting densities, all treatments with 15-ft spacing had similar overall percentages of initial density ranging from 8.5 to 12.8 percent. The plots receiving the 4-ft spacing had the lowest rates (2.5 –3.7%). Due to the uncertainty of the initial planting densities, it is difficult to determine which treatments had an overall better result. However, it is clear that the 4-ft spacing treatments had greater survival from 2008 to 2010, regardless of initial densities. Further testing of these types of treatments is for sagebrush transplant establishment is warranted.

Conclusions

Significant emergence of grasses and forbs occurred at the mid-elevation aerial seedings in 2010, but it is impossible to quantify the proportion of these seedings that were due to the seeding versus naturally occurring. Because densities of emerging seedlings in aerially seeded areas were similar to densities in unseeded areas, enough seed was produced, germinated, and emerged from pre-existing perennial grasses to contribute a substantial amount of seedlings when conditions were appropriate, as they were in spring 2010. These seedlings, regardless of whether they were from existing plants or from the seeding treatments, will have a large amount of competition due to the high densities of pre-existing perennial grasses. Aerially seeding into "closed" communities reduces seedling emergence and establishment because most available suitable microsites are already occupied by live plants or biotic crusts. Historically, emergence and establishment of aerially applied seed has been very low in general due to loss of seed from landing in inadequate microsites, desiccation, wind and water erosion, and predation by rodents and birds (Nelson and others, 1970).

If plant mortality due to the fire were higher, this may have opened up more microsites and caused increased seedling emergence and a greater chance at establishment; however, mortality of existing plants was low. Additionally, within the large area treated by aerially seeding, there may have been locations with lower-than-average pre-existing plants where seedlings were primarily due to the seeding.

At the lower elevation aerial seedings, there was a more limited seed source from pre-existing plants and some emergence due to the treatments likely occurred. Seedlings found in these treatments are more easily attributed to the aerial seedling due to the low densities of pre-existing perennial grasses.

Within drill seedings, a significant amount of seedlings emerged in 2009 and 2010, ranging from 0.13 to 1.40 in 2009, and 1.90 to 5.90 grass seedlings/m^2 in 2010. The drill seedings resulted in some germination even in 2009, a drought year, when no-drill plots had no seedlings, and significant germination in 2010, a year when no-drill plots showed some seedling emergence. These emerging seedlings will have reduced competition from the low densities of pre-existing perennial grasses, but potentially higher competition from exotic annual grasses and forbs as their populations fluctuate over time. Therefore, it is unclear how many of these seedlings will ultimately survive. Intermediate and long-term success of these treatments should be assessed by future monitoring and comparison to the no-drill plots.

Although the effect of the herbicides Plateau® (Imazapic) and Journey® (Imazapic + glyphosate) are difficult to quantify because they were applied prior to the beginning of monitoring, it is apparent that there was a profound effect on the dominance of *B. tectorum* (and indirectly, *S. kali*) in areas where these species were abundant before treatment. In areas with shifting soils (sand dunes), fire combined with herbicide treatment that drastically reduced *B. tectorum* cover and density may have facilitated mortality of shallow-rooted perennial grasses and loss of soil due to wind. The effect is less clear in aerially seeded areas that had high densities of existing perennial grasses, although reduced *B. tectorum* density and cover did occur in these areas as well. The variability seen in densities of *S. kali* may be due to the herbicide banding. Areas that appeared to have a great amount of *S. kali* and a potential loss of *P. secunda* may have been areas that received more than the prescribed herbicide rate because of drift of the herbicide. This may have created areas where all *B. tectorum* were removed, and the shallow-rooted perennial grasses had reduced growth, leading to more available resources for *S. kali*.

Lower densities of *B. tectorum* and *S. kali* combined with adequate moisture, and perhaps reduced cover of existing grasses, combined to create optimal conditions for germination in 2010. There is a natural amount of seedling mortality after emergence, and it is unclear what this amount will be for these treatments, although it is likely to be substantial. Based on some estimates for wetter sites (10–12 in. annual precipitation), approximately 5 plants/m^2 is indicative of a successful seeding in the Intermountain West (Vallentine, 1989). These current sites receive nearly one-half this precipitation, so it is reasonable to expect less plant density from a successful seeding. Therefore, drill seedings appear to be on track for a successful seeding unless mortality rates become excessive (greater than 75 percent).

The location of transplanting *A. tridentata* (near a wash or an upland area) seemed to affect survival the greatest, with survival rates from 46 to 76 percent. Within the upland areas, all treatments showed similar survival, but further study is warranted. Information on planting locations, microsites, and other treatments to increase transplant survival of *A. tridentata* is needed as the area occupied by this species decreases due to wildfires, such as on ALE.

Overall, the seedings following the Milepost 17 and Wautoma fires demonstrate that significant germination can occur given proper seeding methods and favorable weather conditions, despite low elevation and low average annual precipitation (6.8 inches). Additionally, knowledge regarding pre-fire vegetation and accurate estimates of post-fire mortality are critical for land managers when deciding when and where to seed. Pre-fire plant communities affected by the Wautoma and Milepost 17 fires were well known, but the level of possible mortality was not. Within the burned area, there was very little mortality of pre-existing plants due to the fire, despite estimates that mortality would be high. Research is needed on quick and reliable methods to predict mortality of pre-fire plants in these upland areas to aid resource allocation after wildfires. In general, treatments with high amounts of pre-existing grasses are able to reseed themselves given favorable climate and probably do not need to be seeded unless they have lost key species, such as sagebrush. For these areas that are lacking primarily sagebrush, but have a relatively intact understory of native perennials, an alternative to transplanting may be to seed in multiple years to increase the chance that conditions will be conducive to plant establishment.

Acknowledgments

The U.S. Fish and Wildlife Service Columbia River National Refuge Complex provided the funding for this work (Agreement #135808H344). We would specifically like to thank Heidi Newsome, Kevin Goldie, and Greg Hughes from USFWS. We also would like to thank USGS staff that have helped with fieldwork, offered advice, and assisted with report preparation including: Kevin Knutson, Meagan Gates, Peter Del Zotto, Georjanna Pokorney, Andrew Lindgren, Nicole DeCrappeo, Scott Shaff, Susan Powell, Janet Erickson, Ruth Jacobs, and Sue Phillips. Additional thanks to Lisa Ganio and Manuela Huso for statistical advice.

References Cited

Baker, W.L., Garner, J., Lyon, P. 2009, Effect of imazapic on cheatgrass and native plants in Wyoming big sagebrush restoration for Gunnison sage-grouse. Natural Areas Journal, v. 29, p. 204-209.

Bekedam, S., 2004, Establishment tolerance of six native sagebrush steppe species to imazapic (PLATEAU®) herbicide: Implications for restoration and recovery: Corvallis, Oregon, Oregon State University, M.S. Thesis, 93 p.

Brown, R., 1995, The water relations of range plants: Adaptations to water deficits, *in* Bedunah, D., and Sosebee, R.E., eds., Rangeland Plant Physiology and Morphology: Denver, CO, Society for Range Management, 710 p.

Evans, J.R., and Lih, M.P., 2005, Recovery and rehabilitation of vegetation on the Fitzner-Eberhardt arid lands Ecology reserve, Hanford Reach National Monument, following the 24 Command fire, Final Report 2001-2004: Seattle, WA, The Nature Conservancy of Washington, 254 p.

First Strike Environmental, 2007a, Wautoma Fire Burned Area Emergency Response Plan: Roseburg, OR, U.S. Fish and Wildlife Service Report, 173 p.

First Strike Environmental, 2007b, Wautoma Fire Burned Area Emergency Response Plan: Roseburg, OR, U.S. Fish and Wildlife Service Report, 129 p.

Herrick, J.E., Van Zee, J.W., Havstad, K.M., Burkett, L.M., and Whitford, W.G., 2005, Monitoring manual for grassland, shrubland and savanna ecosystems Volume 1: Quick Start: USDA – ARS Jornada Experimental Range: Las Cruces, New Mexico, 36 p.

Kyser, G.B., DiTomaso, J.M., Doran, M.P., Orloff, S.B., Wilson, R.G., Lancaster, D.L., Lile, D.F., and Porath, M.L., 2007, Control of medusahead (*Taeniatherum caput-medusae*) and other annual grasses with imazapic: Weed Technology, v. 21, p. 66-75.

Morris, C., Monaco, T.A., and Rigby, C.W. 2009. Variable impacts of imazapic rate on downy brome (*Bromus tectorum*) and seeded species in two rangeland communities. Invasive Plant Science and Management, v. 2, p. 110-119.

Nelson, J.R., Wilson, A., and Goebel, C., 1970, Factors influencing broadcast seeding in bunchgrass range: Journal of Range Management, v. 23, p. 163-170.

R Development Core Team, 2010, R: A language and environment for statistical computing: Vienna, Austria, R Foundation for Statistical Computing, available only online at http://www.R-project.org.

Shinn, S.L., and Thill, D.C., 2004, Tolerance of several perennial grasses to imazapic: Weed Technology, v. 18, p. 60-65.

Tu, M., Hurd, C., and Randall, J.M., 2001, Weed Control Methods Handbook, The Nature Conservancy, available only online at http://tncinvasives.ucdavis.edu.

Vallentine, J.F., 1971, Range development and improvements: Provo, Utah, Brigham Young University Press, 524 p.

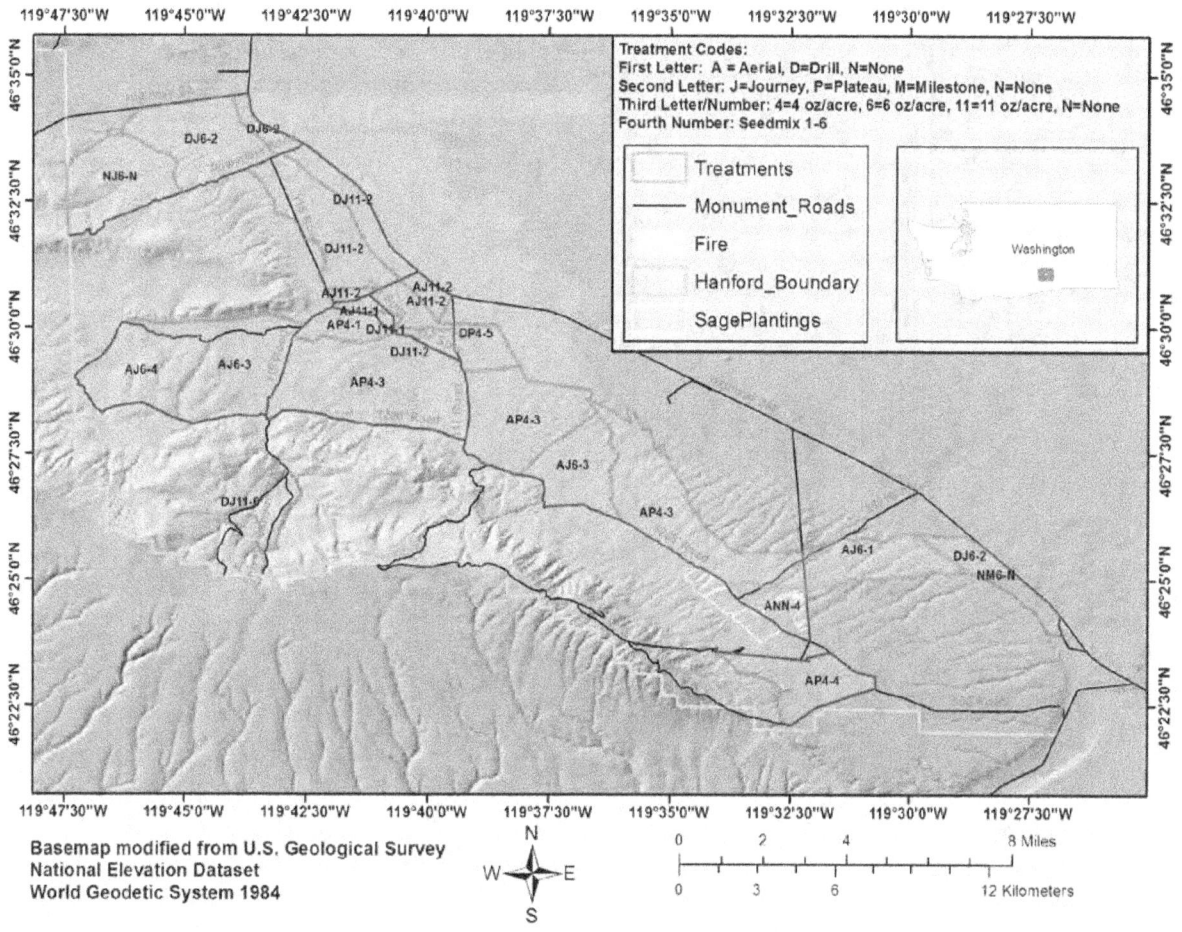

Figure 1. Location of Fitzner-Eberhardt Arid Land Ecology Reserve, Washington, and treatments applied following the Milepost 17 and Wautoma fires of 2007. Coordinates are in North American Datum 1983, Universal Transverse Mercator Zone 11 North.

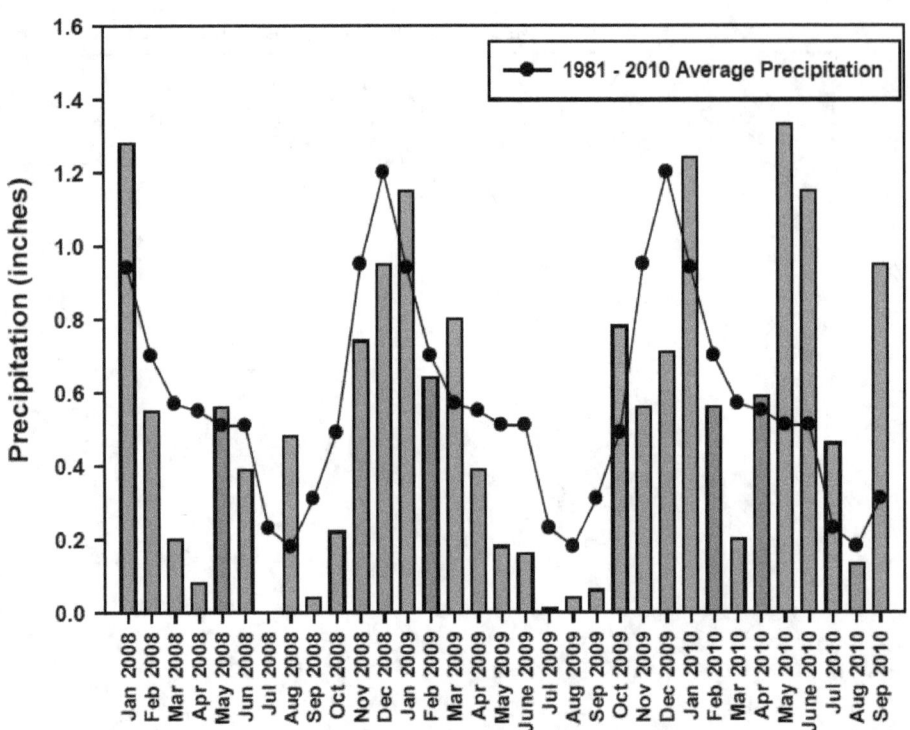

Figure 2. Precipitation received at the Hanford meteorological station from January 2008 to September 2010. Purple bars indicate months that received 80–120 percent of normal precipitation, green bars received greater than 120 percent average precipitation and orange bars indicate months that received less than 80 percent average precipitation.

Figure 3. Monitoring photographs of (a) boundary of fire showing increased movement of soil due to wind in the herbicide treated area, while non-herbicided area dominated by cheatgrass stabilizes the soil but is not conducive to seedling germination and establishment, (b) mortality of *P. secunda* due to wind erosion, (c) banding of areas dominated by *S. kali* and *B.tectorum*/perennial grasses, and (d) apparent *P. secunda* mortality within banding.

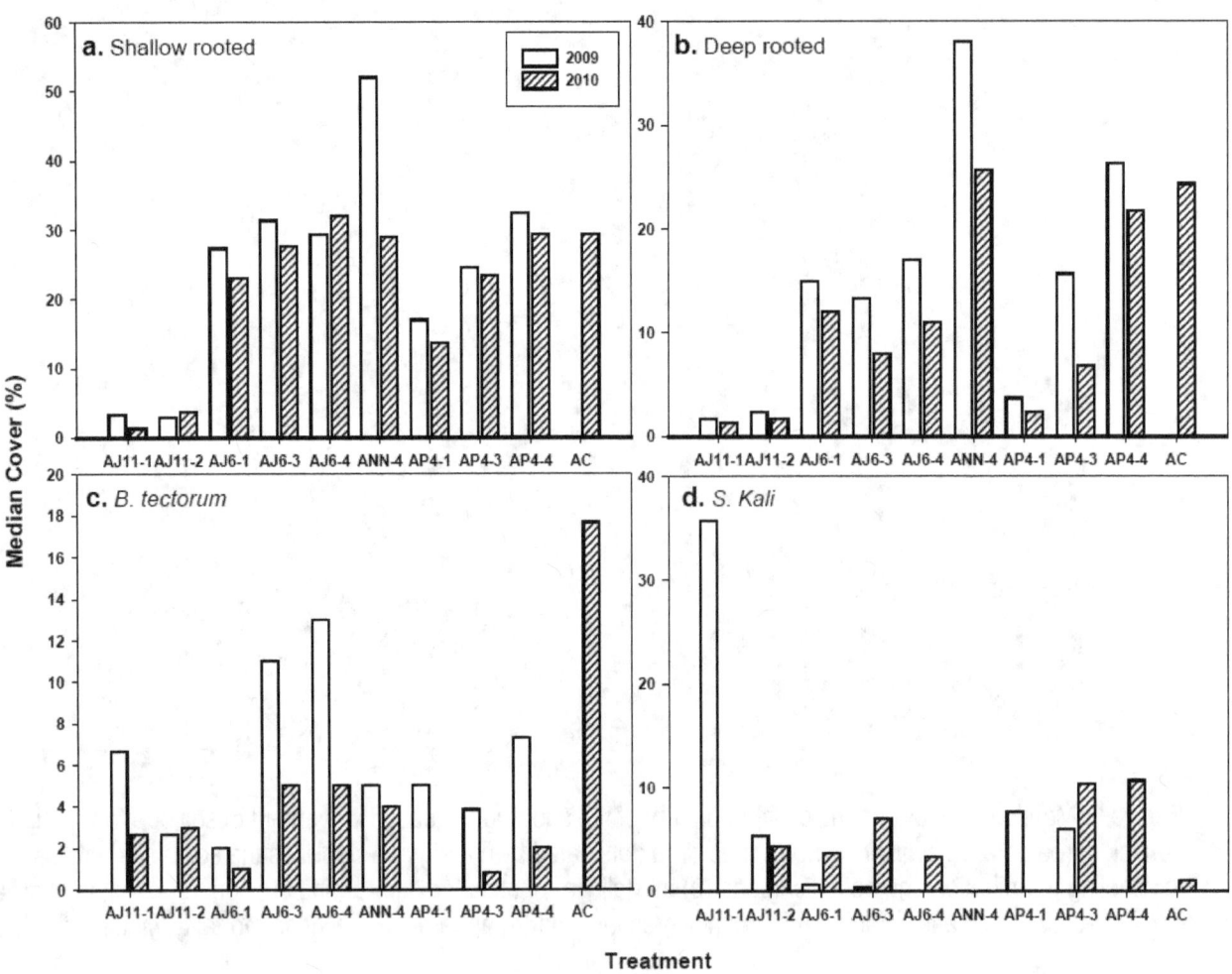

Figure 4. Median cover of (a) shallow-rooted perennial grasses, (b) deep-rooted perennial grasses, (c) *B. tectorum*, and (d) *S. kali* at the aerially seeded plots, Fitzner-Eberhardt Arid Land Ecology Reserve, Washington, 2009–2010. See figure 1 for treatment codes. Note different scales on the Y-axes.

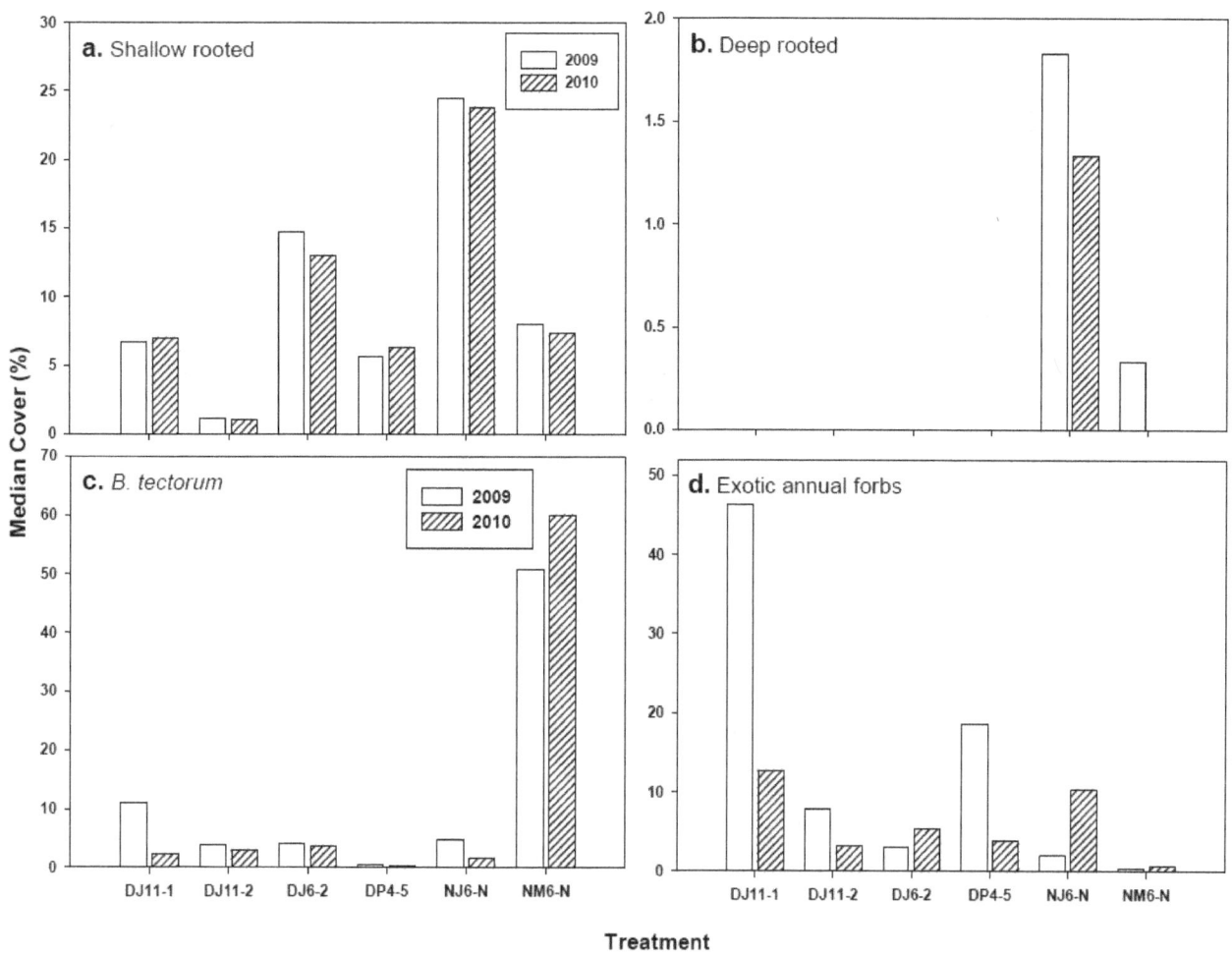

Figure 5. Median cover of (a) shallow rooted perennial grasses, (b) deep rooted perennial grasses, (c) Exotic annual grasses (*B. tectorum*), and (d) exotic annual forbs at the drill seeding sites (control and treatments plots combined), Fitzner-Eberhardt Arid Land Ecology Reserve, Washington. See figure 1 for treatment codes. Note different scales on the Y-axes.

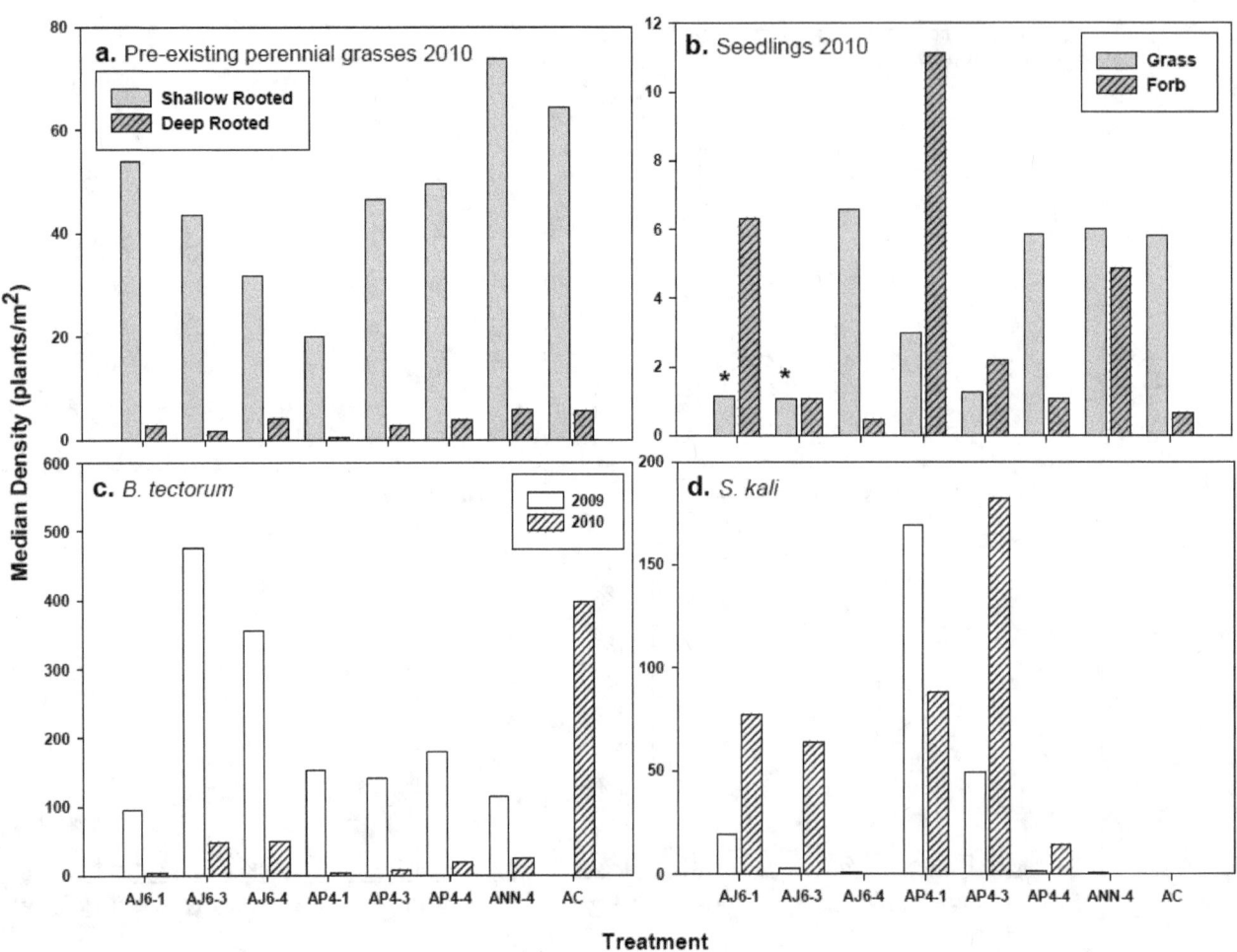

Figure 6. Median density (a) existing deep and shallow rooted perennial grasses, (b) seedling grass and forbs, (c) *B. tectorum*, and (d) *S. kali* at the mid-elevation aerially seeded treatments in 2009 and 2010 following the 2007 wildfires at the Arid Land Ecology Reserve, Washington. See figure 1 for treatment codes. Note different scales on y-axes.

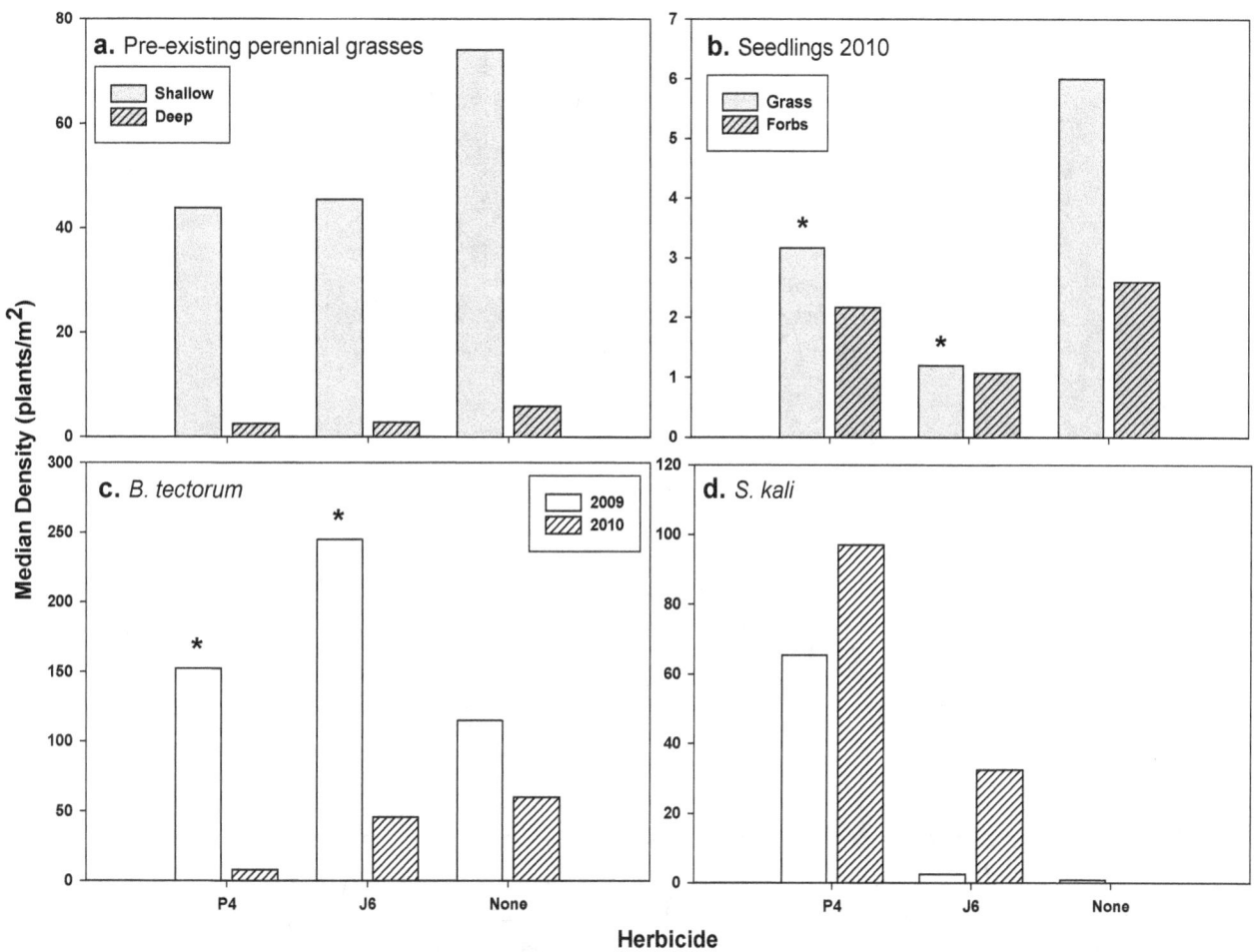

Figure 7. Median density of (a) pre-existing deep and shallow rooted perennial grasses, (b) seedling grass and forbs, (c) *B. tectorum*, and (d) *S. kali* by herbicide at the mid-elevation aerially seeded sites following the 2007 wildfires at the Fitzner-Eberhardt Arid Land Ecology Reserve, Washington, 2009–10. See figure 1 for treatment codes. Asterisks denote significant differences between treatment compared to no treatment. Note different scales on y-axes.

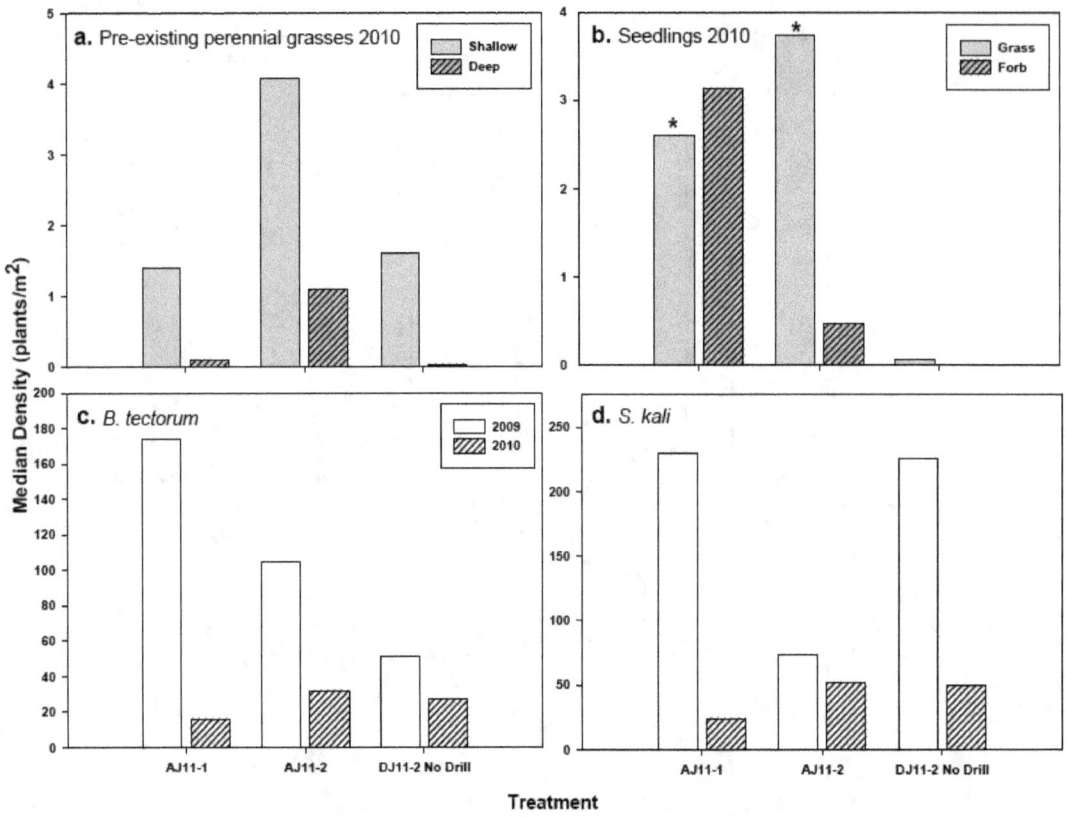

Figure 8. Median density of (a) pre-existing shallow and deep-rooted perennial grasses, (b) seedling grasses, (c) *B. tectorum*, and (d) *S. kali* at the low-elevation aerial seeding treatments and DJ11-2 no-drill plots (DJ11-2 C) following the 2007 wildfires at the Fitzner-Eberhardt Arid Land Ecology Reserve, Washington, 2009–10. See figure 1 for treatment codes. Note different scales on the y-axes. Asterisks denote a significant difference between the DJ11-2 no-drill plots.

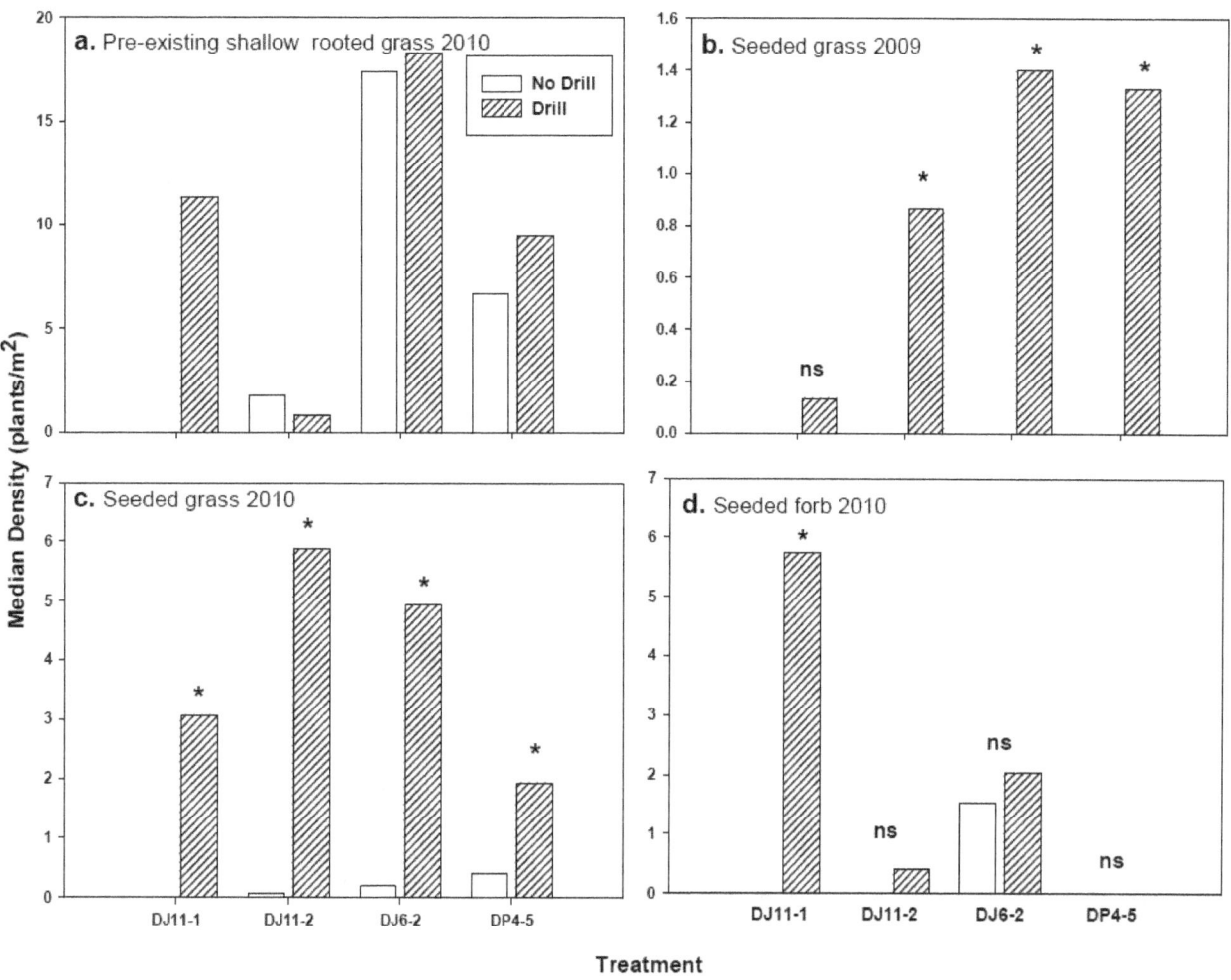

Figure 9. Median density of (a) pre-existing shallow-rooted perennial grasses, (b) seeded grasses in 2009, (c) seeded grasses in 2010, and (d) seeded forbs in 2010 by treatment at the low elevation drill seeding no-drill and treatment plots following the 2007 wildfires at the Fitzner-Eberhardt Arid Land Ecology Reserve, Washington, 2009–10. Note different scales on the y-axes. Asterisks denote significant differences between no-drill and treatment plots for seeded grass and forbs while "ns" denotes non-significance.

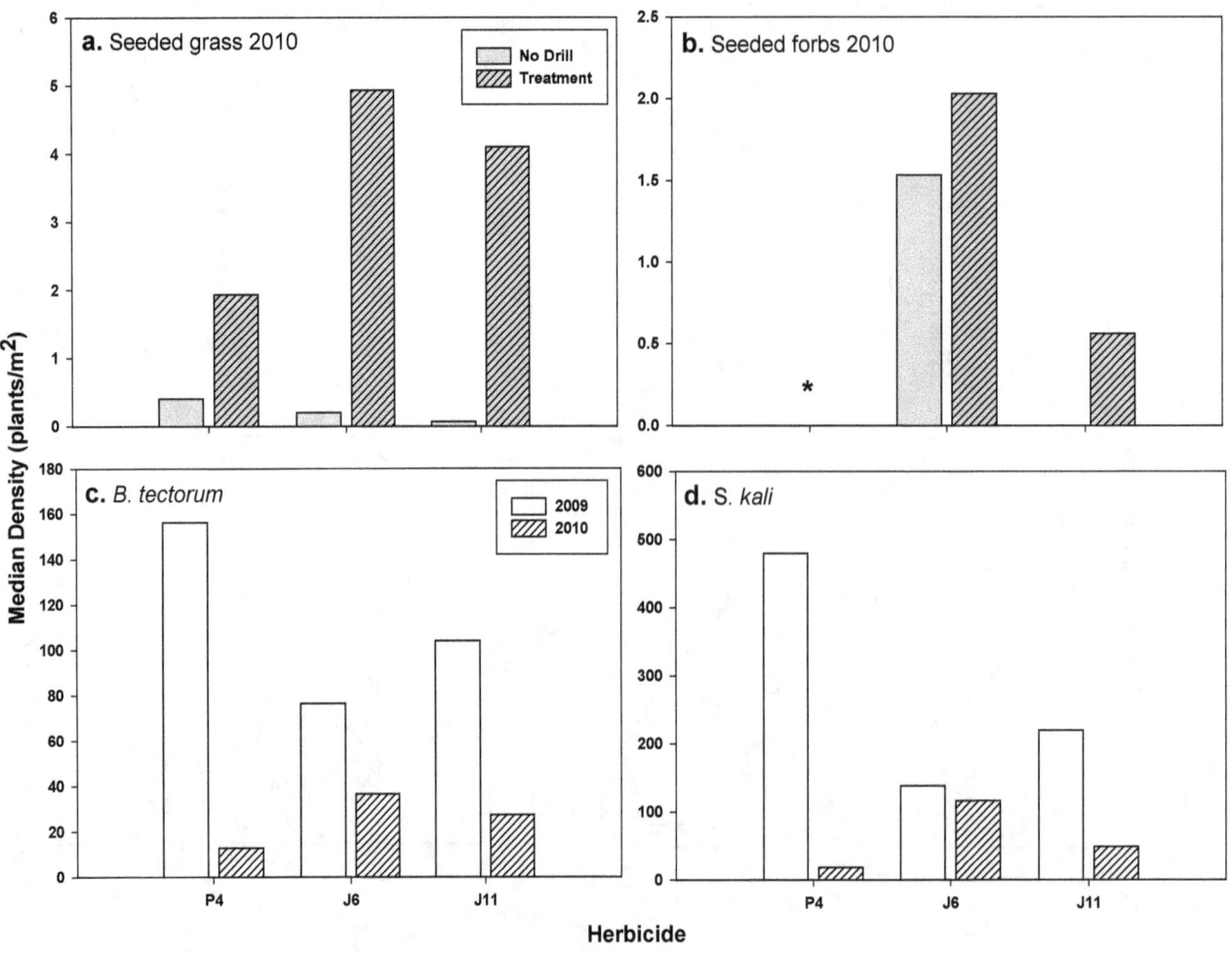

Figure 10. Median density of (a) seeded grasses, (b) seeded forbs at the control and treatment plots and (c) *B. tectorum*, and (d) *S. kali* by herbicide at the low elevation drill seeding treatment plots following the 2007 wildfires at the Fitzner-Eberhardt Arid Land Ecology Reserve, Washington, 2009–10. See figure 1 for treatment codes. Asterisks denote significant differences between treatments. Note different scales on the Y-axes.

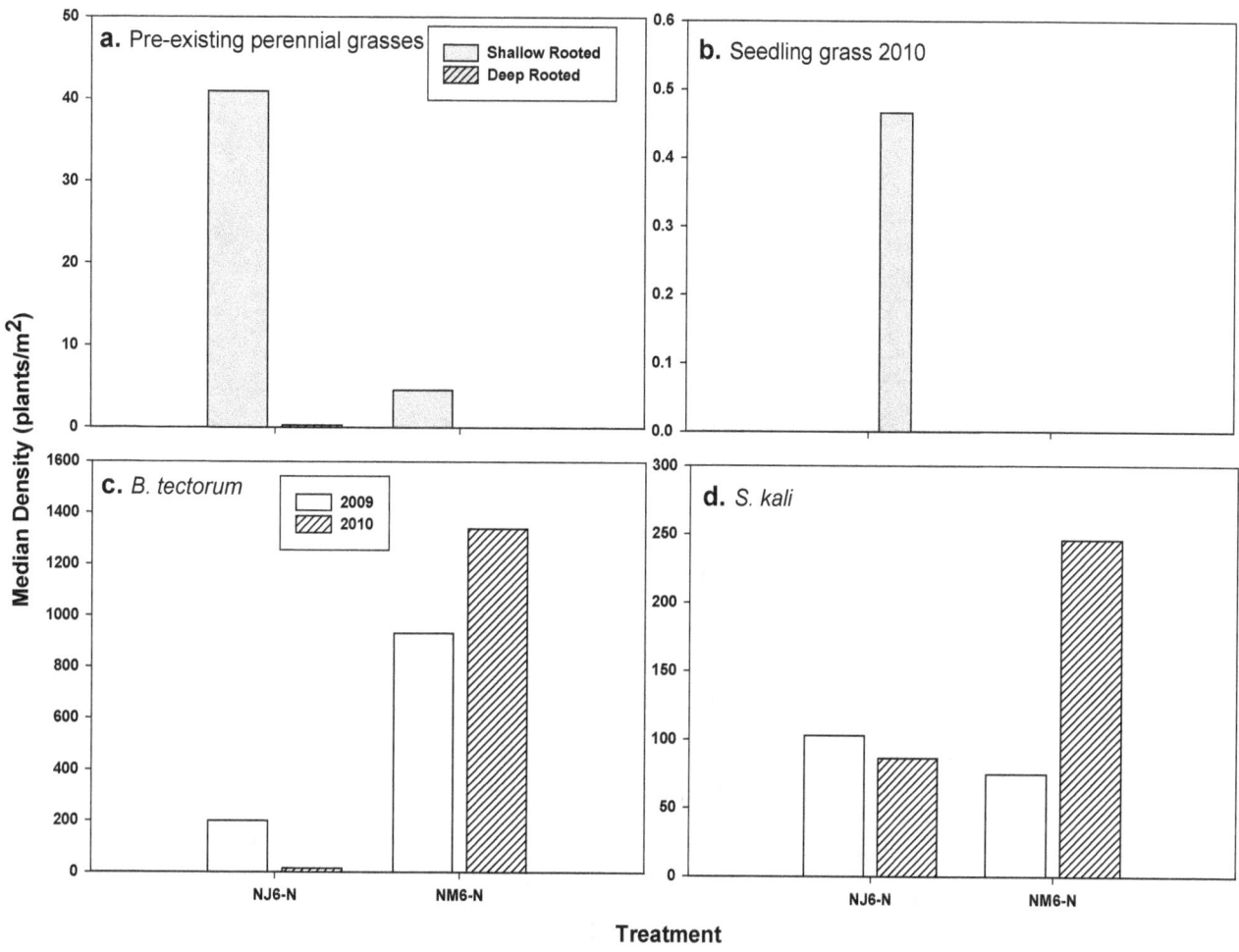

Figure 11. Median density of (a) shallow and deep rooted perennial grasses, (b) seedling grass, (c) *B. tectorum*, and (d) *S. kali* by treatment at the no seeding treatments following the 2007 wildfires at the Fitzner-Eberhardt Arid Land Ecology Reserve, Washington, 2009–10. See figure 1 for treatment codes. Note different scales on the Y-axes.

Table 1. Seeding and herbicide treatments applied following the Wautoma and Milepost 17 wildfires at the Fitzner-Eberhardt Arid Land Ecology Reserve, Washington.

[Number of plots: Number before and after the comma (,) is treatment, no-drill plots. oz/acre, ounce per acre]

Treatment code	Seeding type	Herbicide	Herbicide rate oz/acre	Seedmix	Seeding date	Herbicide date	Acres	Number of plots
AJ11-1	Aerial	Journey	11	1	11/08	3/08	131	3
AJ11-2	Aerial	Journey	11	2	11/08	3/08	818	5
AJ6-1	Aerial	Journey	6	1	11/08	3/08	1434	5
AJ6-3	Aerial	Journey	6	3	11/08	3/08	3760	11
AP4-1	Aerial	Plateau	4	1	11/08	3/08	533	3
AP4-3	Aerial	Plateau	4	3	11/08	3/08	8719	14
AP4-4	Aerial	Plateau	4	4	11/08	3/08	1300	5
ANN-4	Aerial	None	None	4	11/08	na	610	5
AC	Aerial	None	None	None	na	na	na	6
DP4-5	Drill	Plateau	4	5	11/08-2/09	3/08	567	3, 3
DJ6-2	Drill	Journey	6	2	11/08-2/09	3/08	2725	7, 8
DJ11-1	Drill	Journey	11	1	11/08-2/09	3/08	62	3
DJ11-2	Drill	Journey	11	2	11/08-2/09	3/08	2938	11, 9
DJ11-6	Drill	Journey	11	6	11/09	3/08	704	3
NJ6-N	None	Journey	6	None	na	3/08	1851	6
NM6-N	None	Milestone	6	None	na	3/08	810	3

28

Table 2. Seedmixes applied following the Wautoma and Milepost 17 wildfires at the Fitzner-Eberhardt Arid Land Ecology Reserve, Washington.

Species	Rate (pure live seed lbs/acre)					
	Sandy/loamy low-elevation soils		Silty/loamy mid-elevation soils			Seedmix 6 High elevation soils
	Seedmix 1	Seedmix 2	Seedmix 3	Seedmix 4	Seedmix 5	
Achnatherum hymenoides 'Nezpar' (Roem. & Schult.) Barkworth	3.00	1.50	2.75	1.38	1.38	3.00
Heterostipa comata 'Hanford' (Trin. & Rupr.) Barkworth	0.00	0.00	0.20	0.10	0.10	0.05
Poa secunda 'Hanford' J. Presl	5.00	2.50	3.00	1.50	1.50	3.00
Pseudoroegneria spicata (Pursh) A. Löve	0.00	0.00	3.00	1.50	1.50	3.00
Sporobolus cryptandrus (Torr.) A. Gray	0.50	0.25	0.50	0.25	0.25	0.50
Elymus elymoides (Raf.) Swezey	1.50	0.75	1.25	0.63	0.63	1.00
Elymus lanceolatus 'Schwendimar' (Scribn. & J.G. Sm.) Gould	0.00	0.00	0.00	0.00	0.00	0.00
Achillea millefolium L. var. *occidentalis* DC.	0.30	0.15	0.30	0.15	0.15	0.30
Linum perenne L.	0.30	0.15	0.30	0.15	0.15	0.30
Artemisia tridentata Nutt. ssp. *wyomingensis* Beetle & Young	0.00	0.00	0.10	0.05	0.05	0.10
Krascheninnikovia lanata (Pursh) A. Meeuse & Smit	0.00	0.00	0.10	0.05	0.05	0.10
Purshia tridentata (Pursh) DC.	0.00	0.00	0.00	0.00	0.00	0.10
Leymus cinereus (Scribn. & Merr.) A. Löve	0.00	0.00	0.00	0.00	0.00	4.00
Total pure live seed seeded	**10.60**	**5.30**	**11.50**	**5.76**	**5.80**	**15.50**

Table 3. Target and estimated seeding rates from aerial seeding traps by species (seeds/m²) based on seed traps at the aerially seeded portions of the Wautoma and Milepost 17 wildfires at the Fitzner-Eberhardt Arid Land Ecology Reserve, Washington.

[Numbers in parentheses are 95-percent confidence intervals. Seeds/m², seeds per square meter; na, not applicable]

Species	Mix 1 Target	Mix 1 Traps (n=12)	Mix 2 Target	Mix 2 Traps (n=11)	Mix 3 Target	Mix 3 Traps (n=23)	Mix 4 Target	Mix 4 Traps (n=23)
A. hymenoides	120.0	56.6 (30.2)	60.0	18.21 (12.4)	110.0	49.7 (12.5)	55.2	26.5 (10.1)
A. millefolium	211.4	138.0 (44.1)	105.7	52.9 (60.9)	211.4	167.7 (64.4)	105.7	63.7 (34.4)
A. tridentata ssp. wyomingensis	0.0	0.0 (0.0)	0.0	0.0 (0.0)	42.0	17.7 (9.2)	21.0	5.7 (9.6)
E. elymoides	71.1	29.4 (26.7)	35.6	15.3 (22.5)	59.3	79.7 (28.3)	29.9	18.4 (9.8)
H. comata	0.0	0.0 (0.0)	0.0	0.0 (0.0)	6.8	2.5 (2.1)	3.4	1.5 (1.7)
K. lanata	0.0	0.0 (0.0)	0.0	0.0 (0.0)	2.7	4.5 (2.9)	1.4	3.4 (3.3)
L. perenne	21.9	25.9 (20.6)	10.9	6.1 (5.3)	21.9	27.3 (11.4)	10.9	10.7 (8.4)
P. secunda	1716.6	717.7 (366.6)	858.0	484.0 (370)	1029.9	574.4 (167.2)	515.0	170.8 (94.5)
P. spicata	0.0	0.0 (0.0)	0.0	0.0 (0.0)	93.1	20.2 (8.8)	46.6	4.3 (4.8)
S. cryptandrus	691.7	113.7 (99.0)	345.8	23.9 (25.1)	691.7	258.0 (95.7)	345.8	57.4 (43.7)
Unknown	**na**	39.8 (43.6)	**na**	41.8 (64.2)	**na**	0.9 (1.9)	**na**	4.5 (4.7)
Seeds/m²	**2,832.5**	**1,121.0 (1,146.6)**	**1,416.3**	**642.2 (493.2)**	**2,268.8**	**1,175.6 (330.0)**	**1,134.8**	**366.3 (199.6)**

Table 4. Treatment groupings and statistical comparisons performed for data collected after the Milepost 17 and Wautoma wildfires at the Fitzner-Eberhardt Arid Land Ecology Reserve, Washington.

Group	Treatments included	Plots used for comparison	Technique
Mid-elevation aerial seedings	AJ6-1, AJ6-3, AP4-1, AP4-3, AP4-4	AC	1-way ANOVA followed by Dunnett's test between each treatment and the AC plots
	Journey: AJ6-1, AJ6-3 Plateau : AP4-1, AP4-3, AP4-4	ANN-4	1-way ANOVA followed by Dunnett's test between each herbicide group and ANN-4 plots
Low-elevation aerial seedings	AJ11-1, AJ11-2	DJ11-2 no-drill plots	1-way ANOVA followed by Dunnett's test between each treatment and the DJ11-2 no-drill plots
Low-elevation drill seedings	DJ11-1, DJ11-2, DJ6-2, DP4-5	DJ11-1, DJ11-2, DJ6-2, and DP4-5 no-drill plots	Welch 2-sample t-test between the drill and no drill plots for each treatment
	Journey, Plateau	Each treatment	1-way ANOVA
High-elevation drill seeding	DJ11-6	No comparisons made	na
No seeding	NJ6-N, NM6-N	No comparisons made	na

31

Table 5. Median densities (plants/m^2) of important lifeforms at the Fitzner-Eberhardt Arid Land Ecology Reserve, Washington, 2009–10.

[Drill seedings do not include DJ11-6, which was seeded in 2009. SR = shallow rooted, DR = deep rooted. plants/m^2, plants per square meter]

Treatment	Year	Seeded grass	Seeded forb	Seeded shrub	B. tectorum	S. kali	SR grass	DR grass
Aerial seedings	2009	0.00	0.03	0.00	152.50	24.17	44.40	2.61
	2010	3.07	2.60	0.00	17.08	63.33	42.80	1.88
Aerial control	2010	5.80	0.67	0.00	397.08	0.00	61.47	5.57
Drill seedings (4 Sites)	2009	0.87	0.00	0.00	76.67	200.00	8.86	0.01
	2010	4.20	0.47	0.00	32.50	54.17	3 27	0.01
Drill seeding control (3 Sites)	2009	0.00	0.00	0.00	157.50	225.83	7.00	0.002
	2010	0.13	0.00	0.00	24.17	50.83	6.67	0.002

Table 6. Transplant survival by treatment following the 2007 wildfires at the Fitzner-Eberhardt Arid Land Ecology Reserve, Washington, 2008–10.

Treatment / Site	Initial planting		2008		2009			2010			
	N (t)	Density[1]	Density[2]	$O-t_1$[3]	Density[2]	t_1-t_2[3]	$O-t_2$[3]	Density[2]	t_2-t_3[3]	t_1-t_3[3]	$O-t_3$[3]
Plant Success tablets, 15 ft	5 (3)	0.047	0.021	44.6	0.01	47.6	21.2	0.006	60.0	28.6	12.8
MycoApply root dip, 15 ft	5 (3)	0.047	0.023	48.9	0.007	30.4	14.9	0.005	74.4	21.7	10.6
TerraSorb Medium, 15 ft	15 (3)	0.047	0.016	34.0	0.004	25.0	8.5	0.004	100.0	25.0	8.5
TerraSorb Medium, 4 ft	12 (1)	0.67	0.033	4.9	0.031	93.9	4.6	0.025	80.6	75.8	3.7
Control, 15 ft	5 (3)	0.047	0.020	42.6	0.008	40.0	17.0	0.005	62.5	25.0	10.6
Control, 4 ft	4 (1)	0.67	0.037	5.5	0.024	64.9	3.6	0.017	62.9	45.9	2.5

[1] Plants/m² assumed from initial planting densities.
[2] Plants/m² (measured).
[3] $O-t_1$ = Percent of original density from original planting date to 2008, $O-t_2$ = Percent of original density from original planting date to 2009, t_1-t_2 = Percent of density persisting from 2008 to 2009, t_2-t_3 = Percent of density persisting from 2009 to 2010, t_1-t_3 = Percent of density persisting from 2008 to 2010, $O-t_3$ = Percent of original density persisting to 2010. t = the number of transects per plot.

Appendix A. Plot Data

Table A1. Location and physical characteristics of monitoring plots established following treatments at the Wautoma and Milepost 17 wildfires at the Fitzner-Eberhardt Arid Land Ecology Reserve, Washington.

[Coordinates are in North American Datum 1983, UTM Zone 11, elevation datum is North American Vertical Datum 1988]

Plot	Northing	Easting	Elevation (meters)	Slope (percent)	Aspect	Surface soil texture
AC-1	5143013	303023	383	8	Northeast	Silt Loam
AC-2	5150377	287219	378	5	South	Silt Loam
AC-3	5149665	288784	369	13	West	Silt Loam
AC-4	5147802	296737	350	6	Northeast	Silt Loam
AC-5	5151124	298000	184	2	South	Sand
AC-6	5150990	298505	181	3	North	Silt Loam
AC-7	5152387	286943	270	1	East	Silt Loam
AC-8	5142908	302586	408	7	Northeast	Silt Loam
AJ11-1-T1	5153886	293952	197	6	South	Sand
AJ11-1-T2	5153901	293415	199	1	Northwest	Sand
AJ11-1-T3	5153768	293723	196	2	Northeast	Sand
AJ11-2-T1	5154447	294502	194	1	Northeast	Sand
AJ11-2-T2	5153260	294754	192	1	Southwest	Sand
AJ11-2-T3	5153943	294757	202	3	Northeast	Sand
AJ11-2-T4	5154421	293552	205	2	East	Sand
AJ11-2-T5	5154003	295699	195	1	Northeast	Sand
AJ6-1-T1	5144103	306060	260	3	Northeast	Sand
AJ6-1-T2	5143544	305445	291	5	Northwest	Silt Loam
AJ6-1-T3	5144256	307580	205	7	East	Silt Loam
AJ6-1-T4	5143894	306946	246	7	Northeast	Silt Loam
AJ6-1-T5	5144463	305761	250	11	Northwest	Silt Loam
AJ6-3-T1	5147111	299713	290	4	South	Silt Loam
AJ6-3-T2	5146644	298958	342	5	Northeast	Silt Loam
AJ6-3-T3	5150629	290864	291	2	South	Silt Loam
AJ6-3-T4	5150313	289255	343	14	Northeast	Silt Loam
AJ6-3-T5	5152709	290411	240	1	East	Silt Loam
AJ6-3-T6	5151708	290762	257	5	South	Silt Loam
AJ6-3-T7	5148223	298860	262	9	Northeast	Silt Loam
AJ6-3-T8	5147781	298493	293	8	Northeast	Silt Loam
AJ6-3-T9	5150890	289451	335	9	Southeast	Silt Loam
AJ6-3-T10	5146766	299183	317	9	Northeast	Silt Loam
AJ6-3-T11	5147715	299305	274	7	East	Silt Loam
AJ6-4-T1	5150911	288243	325	8	South	Silt Loam
AJ6-4-T2	5150613	286686	342	4	Northwest	Silt Loam
AJ6-4-T3	5152898	287503	263	6	East	Silt Loam

AJ6-4-T4	5152477	289025	267	7	North	Silt Loam
AJ6-4-T5	5151545	287706	330	17	Northwest	Silt Loam
ANN-4-T1	5143177	303201	369	5	East	Silt Loam
ANN-4-T2	5142726	303631	366	6	Northeast	Silt Loam
ANN-4-T3	5142383	304660	339	4	East	Silt Loam
ANN-4-T4	5143101	304547	334	5	Northwest	Silt Loam
ANN-4-T5	5141707	304582	360	5	Northeast	Silt Loam
AP4-1-T1	5153224	293493	203	4	North	Silt Loam
AP4-1-T2	5153484	293233	206	5	West	Sand
AP4-1-T3	5152979	292329	227	1	Northwest	Silt Loam
AP4-3-T1	5150045	295107	225	6	South	Silt Loam
AP4-3-T10	5150596	291732	287	4	Northwest	Silt Loam
AP4-3-T11	5150596	295825	225	3	Northeast	Silt Loam
AP4-3-T12	5150356	297020	215	9	South	Silt Loam
AP4-3-T13	5150796	293143	259	1	Northeast	Silt Loam
AP4-3-T14	5149199	298689	227	11	Northeast	Silt Loam
AP4-3-T2	5149128	296555	292	7	Northeast	Silt Loam
AP4-3-T3	5148102	297354	308	7	North	Silt Loam
AP4-3-T4	5146496	301502	296	5	East	Silt Loam
AP4-3-T5	5151870	292366	246	2	North	Silt Loam
AP4-3-T6	5143544	303187	355	7	East	Silt Loam
AP4-3-T7	5144441	302231	346	8	North	Silt Loam
AP4-3-T8	5147670	301259	229	9	East	Silt Loam
AP4-3-T9	5144100	303199	333	5	East	Silt Loam
AP4-4-T1	5140360	303662	500	14	Northeast	Silt Loam
AP4-4-T2	5139798	304820	398	6	Northeast	Silt Loam
AP4-4-T3	5140038	305940	346	2	East	Silt Loam
AP4-4-T4	5139230	305367	374	5	East	Silt Loam
AP4-4-T5	5139305	305984	360	5	Northeast	Silt Loam
DJ11-1-T1	5153286	294354	193	1	East	Silt Loam
DJ11-1-T2	5153555	294324	192	1	Southeast	Sand
DJ11-1-T3	5153657	293892	196	2	Southeast	Silt Loam
DJ11-2-C1	5158519	291993	204	1	East	Sand
DJ11-2-C2	5152260	295860	185	0	Northeast	Silt Loam
DJ11-2-C3	5155330	293690	199	1	Northeast	Sand
DJ11-2-C4	5154809	294074	198	3	Northeast	Sand
DJ11-2-C5	5155150	293048	201	2	East	Sand
DJ11-2-C6	5157251	293032	193	0	East	Sand
DJ11-2-C7	5156715	292667	198	2	East	Sand
DJ11-2-C8	5157965	292251	198	1	East	Sand
DJ11-2-C9	5156054	293309	195	1	Northeast	Sand
DJ11-2-T1	5154995	294099	191	1	Northeast	Sand
DJ11-2-T2	5158062	292389	200	1	South	Silt Loam

DJ11-2-T3	5152741	295068	188	0	Northeast	Silt Loam
DJ11-2-T4	5158925	292108	205	0	East	Silt Loam
DJ11-2-T5	5158406	292459	201	1	East	Sand
DJ11-2-T6	5155509	293258	198	1	West	Sand
DJ11-2-T7	5156853	293199	196	0	Southeast	Sand
DJ11-2-T8	5157845	292969	196	0	East	Silt Loam
DJ11-2-T9	5154833	293455	200	1	Northeast	Sand
DJ11-2-T10	5154876	293028	206	1	North	Sand
DJ11-2-T11	5157119	292478	193	1	Northeast	Silt Loam
DJ11-6-T1	5145892	290954	587	5	West	Silt Loam
DJ11-6-T2	5146851	291075	515	15	Northwest	Silt Loam
DJ11-6-T3	5146908	290552	545	8	Northeast	Silt Loam
DJ6-2-C1	5144571	308913	148	1	Northeast	Sand
DJ6-2-C2	5144337	309432	146	0	Southwest	Sand
DJ6-2-C3	5143862	309856	143	2	East	Sand
DJ6-2-C4	5160412	289544	236	2	East	Silt Loam
DJ6-2-C5	5160689	290376	224	1	East	Silt Loam
DJ6-2-C6	5160635	288136	248	1	Southeast	Silt Loam
DJ6-2-C7	5161059	288984	251	4	Northeast	Sand
DJ6-2-C8	5159047	289399	262	4	East	Silt Loam
DJ6-2-T1	5159847	289189	250	5	Northeast	Silt Loam
DJ6-2-T2	5158777	289273	280	10	Northeast	Silt Loam
DJ6-2-T3	5144485	309216	148	1	East	Sand
DJ6-2-T4	5144299	309752	145	1	Southeast	Sand
DJ6-2-T5	5160886	290434	232	4	South	Sand
DJ6-2-T6	5160559	289086	241	2	East	Silt Loam
DJ6-2-T7	5159981	290935	218	1	East	Silt Loam
DP4-5-C1	5152643	296225	183	0	Northeast	Silt Loam
DP4-5-C2	5152770	296885	181	0	South	Sand
DP4-5-C3	5151895	296996	182	1	East	Sand
DP4-5-T1	5152733	296622	182	0	East	Sand
DP4-5-T2	5152376	296344	184	1	Northeast	Sand
DP4-5-T3	5152257	297323	184	1	Northeast	Sand
NJ6-N-T1	5159685	287172	299	6	East	Silt Loam
NJ6-N-T2	5159264	286570	343	7	North	Silt Loam
NJ6-N-T3	5159107	287993	283	4	Northeast	Silt Loam
NJ6-N-T4	5158336	287875	318	3	South	Silt Loam
NJ6-N-T5	5158279	286461	396	14	East	Silt Loam
NJ6-N-T6	5157424	286484	370	5	South	Silt Loam
NM6-N-T1	5141616	311598	159	5	Northwest	Sand
NM6-N-T2	5143005	310709	159	1	North	Sand
NM6-N-T3	5142480	311025	141	0	North	Sand

Table A2. Median densities (plants/m²) of important lifeforms at the ALE Aerial seedings in 2009 and 2010.

SD = seedling, SR = shallow rooted, DR = deep rooted, PG = perennial grass, BRTE = *B. tectorum*, SAKA = *S. Kali.*

Site	Year	SD_Grass	SD_Forb	SD_Shrub	BRTE	SAKA	SR_PG	DR_PG
AC	2010	5.80	0.67	0.00	397.08	0.00	61.46	5.57
AJ11-1	2009	0.00	0.00	0.00	174.17	230.00	3.40	0.09
	2010	2.60	3.13	0.00	15.83	24.17	1.40	0.09
AJ11-2	2009	0.27	0.00	0.00	105.00	73.33	3.67	1.36
	2010	3.73	0.47	0.00	31.67	51.67	4.07	1.09
AJ6-1	2009	0.067	0.80	0.00	95.00	19.17	54.00	2.62
	2010	1.13	6.33	0.00	3.33	77.50	54.00	2.75
AJ6-3	2009	0.00	0.07	0.00	475.83	2.50	43.40	2.60
	2010	1.07	1.07	0.00	48.33	64.17	43.4	1.60
AJ6-4	2009	0.00	0.00	0.00	355.00	0.83	41.80	4.05
	2010	6.60	0.47	0.00	49.17	0.00	31.73	4.11
ANN-4	2009	0.07	0.13	0.00	115.00	0.83	74.00	5.83
	2010	6.00	4.87	0.00	24.17	0.00	74.00	5.83
AP4-1	2009	0.00	0.00	0.00	152.50	169.17	19.60	0.82
	2010	3.00	11.13	0.73	3.33	88.33	20.13	0.29
AP4-3	2009	0.00	0.00	0.00	142.08	49.17	49.00	4.22
	2010	1.27	0.38	0.00	7.91	182.08	46.70	2.78
AP4-4	2009	0.00	0.13	0.00	180.00	1.67	50.60	4.14
	2010	5.87	0.20	0.00	18.33	14.17	49.60	3.87

Table A3. Median densities (plants/m^2) of important lifeforms at the ALE drill seeding treatment and controls in 2009 and 2010.

SD = seedling, SR = shallow rooted, DR = deep rooted, PG = perennial grass, BRTE = *B. tectorum*, SAKA = *S. Kali*.

Site	Year	SD_GRASS	SD_Forb	SD_Shrub	BRTE	SAKA	SR_PG	DR_PG
DJ11-1 Treatment	2009	0.133	0.00	0.00	156.67	394.17	12.53	0.00
	2010	3.07	5.73	0.07	27 50	124.17	11.33	0.00
DJ11-2 No-drill	2009	0.00	0.00	0.00	50.83	225.83	1.60	0.03
	2010	0.07	0.00	0.00	26.67	49.17	1.800	0.03
DJ11-2 Treatment	2009	0.87	0.00	0.00	104.17	200.00	0.67	0.01
	2010	5.87	0.40	0.00	63 33	46.67	0.80	0.01
DJ6-2 No-drill	2009	0.00	0.00	0.00	157.50	78.33	19.67	0.00
	2010	0.20	1.53	0.13	19 17	124.17	17.40	0.00
DJ6-2 Treatment	2009	1.40	0.00	0.00	63 33	148.33	18.23	0.01
	2010	4.93	2.03	0.00	49 17	89.17	18.30	0.01
DP4-5 No-drill	2009	0.00	0.00	0.00	273.33	560.00	6.33	0.00
	2010	0.40	0.00	0.00	24 17	9.17	6.67	0.00
DP4-5 Treatment	2009	1.33	0.00	0.00	39 17	399.17	8.87	0.01
	2010	1.93	0.00	0.00	7 50	32.50	9.47	0.01
NJ6-N Treatment	2009	0.00	0.00	0.00	199.17	102.92	41.06	0.25
	2010	0.47	0.00	0.00	14 58	86.25	40.93	0.25
NM6-N Treatment	2009	0.00	0.00	0.00	932.5	75.00	3.86	0.05
	2010	0.00	0.00	0.00	1339.17	245.83	4.53	0.05
DJ11-6 Treatment	2010	60 93	48.8	0.00	165.83	0.00	11.87	0.00

Table A4. Cover of important lifeforms at the ALE Aerial seedings in 2009 and 2010.

EAG = Exotic annual grasses, EAF = Exotic annual forbs, SR_PG = Shallow-rooted perennial grasses,
DR_PG = Deep-rooted perennial grasses, L = Litter, BSC = Biological soil crust (visible), Bare = Bare ground.

Site	Year	EAG	EAF	SR_PG	DR_PG	L	BSC	Bare
AC	2010	17.67	0.00	29.33	24.33	62.67	7.17	9.5
AJ11-1	2009	6.67	35.67	3.67	1.67	34.00	1.67	36.0
	2010	2.67	4.33	1.33	1.33	26.00	1.67	32.00
AJ11-2	2009	2.67	5.33	3.00	2.33	27.00	0.00	51.00
	2010	3.00	3.67	3.66	1.67	24.67	0.00	63.00
AJ6-1	2009	2.00	0.67	27.33	15.00	23.33	0.33	36.00
	2010	1.00	7.00	23.00	12.00	36.67	2.67	22.33
AJ6-3	2009	11.00	0.33	31.33	13.33	45.00	2.67	16.00
	2010	5.00	3.33	27.67	8.00	48.67	10.67	19.66
AJ6-4	2009	13.00	0.00	29.33	17.00	37.67	0.33	21.00
	2010	5.00	0.00	32.00	11.00	53.33	2.00	16.33
ANN-4	2009	5.00	0.00	52.00	38.00	29.00	19.67	8.66
	2010	4.00	0.00	29.00	25.67	37.67	33.67	13.00
AP4-1	2009	5.00	7.67	17.00	3.67	37.00	1.33	40.33
	2010	0.00	10.33	13.67	2.33	35.00	2.00	46.66
AP4-3	2009	3.83	6.00	24.50	15.67	32.67	3.67	31.30
	2010	0.83	10.67	23.33	6.83	43.17	6.67	29.83
AP4-4	2009	7.33	0.00	32.33	26.33	37.67	1.67	23.66
	2010	2.00	1.00	29.33	21.67	47.33	4.33	20.00

Table A5. Cover of important lifeforms at the ALE drill seedings in 2009 and 2010.

[EAG = Exotic annual grasses, EAF = Exotic annual forbs, SR_PG = Shallow-rooted perennial grasses,
DR_PG = Deep-rooted perennial grasses, L = Litter, BSC = Biological soil crust (visible), Bare = Bare ground]

Site	Year	EAG	EAF	SR_PG	DR_PG	L	BSC	Bare
DJ11-1 Treatment	2009	11.00	46.33	6.67	0.00	30.33	0.00	31.66
	2010	2.33	12.67	7.00	0.00	20.67	0.00	66.66
DJ11-2 Control	2009	3.67	9.33	2.67	1.00	28.67	0.00	53.66
	2010	1.67	2.33	2.33	0.33	34.33	0.00	54.33
DJ11-2 Treatment	2009	4.00	7.33	0.33	0.00	26.67	0.00	59.33
	2010	4.67	4.67	0.67	0.00	36.67	0.00	51.66
DJ11-6 Treatment	2010	12.33	0.00	3.67	0.00	68.67	0.00	19.66
DJ6-2 Control	2009	6.00	7.33	14.67	0.17	28.00	0.67	45.17
	2010	3.00	9.00	13.00	0.00	39.33	0.33	41.33
DJ6-2 Treatment	2009	2.17	2.50	15.00	0.00	19.67	0.00	54.66
	2010	3.83	4.17	16.00	0.00	30.00	0.00	44.33
DP4-5 Control	2009	4.00	18.00	6.67	0.33	36.00	0.00	52.00
	2010	0.33	3.67	5.33	0.00	31.00	0.00	60.00
DP4-5 Treatment	2009	0.00	22.67	4.67	0.00	25.33	0.00	44.33
	2010	0.33	4.00	7.33	0.00	25.33	0.33	62.00
NJ6-N Treatment	2009	4.67	2.00	24.50	1.83	38.5	0.67	33.83
	2010	1.66	10.33	23.83	1.33	33.83	7.33	40.50
NM6-N Treatment	2009	50.67	0.33	8.00	0.33	88.67	1.00	5.66
	2010	60.00	0.67	7.33	0.00	88.33	2.67	8.00

www.ingramcontent.com/pod-product-compliance
Lightning Source LLC
Chambersburg PA
CBHW080344290526
45791CB00009BA/2723